Gifts That Differ:
Lay Ministries Established and Unestablished

*Studies in the Reformed Rites
of the Catholic Church,
Volume VIII*

David N. Power, O.M.I.

Gifts That Differ:

Lay Ministries
Established and Unestablished

Pueblo Publishing Company

New York

Design: Frank Kacmarcik

Much of the material in Chapter Seven originally appeared in an article in *Worship,* May 1978. Thanks are due to the editor for his permission to use the material.

Printed in the United States of America.

ISBN: 0-916134-43-1

Contents

The Ongoing Present

Introduction

In 1972, Pope Paul VI set up the two offices of acolyte and reader as official lay ministries, and in 1973 the Congregation for the Discipline of Sacraments issued norms for the appointment of special ministers of the eucharist. These dispositions were intended to follow up on the principles of the Second Vatican Council concerning the participation of the baptized in the life of the church, and in the liturgy in particular. In practice, outside seminaries one seldom meets a person who has been installed as either acolyte or reader, and the sporadic attempts, even in the highest circles, to restrict the participation of women in eucharistic ministry has become a nagging feature of church life. Yet lay ministries, liturgical and other, thrive, and installation ceremonies of one kind or another, provided for in no official book, are common.

The new offices of acolyte and reader thus hold an ambiguous place in liturgical reform. When Pueblo Publishing Company projected a series of books explaining the new rites, which would not include ordination, the question was raised whether and how a commentary on these lay offices and their liturgies should be included. I accepted the challenge to write this book on the understanding that the official position of the Holy See demanded a fuller consideration of lay ministries, their nature, their origin, their installation and recognition. The work would need to take into account the wide spectrum of lay activity in the church, to see this in its present context, and to relate it to history.

It would be foolish to try to resolve all the theological niceties in such a way as to monitor developments too closely. The Holy Spirit is not so readily trammeled. Some reflection, however, seems appropriate and the situation is mature enough to warrant it. What I offer in this work is based on history, recent theological developments, and current practice around the world. Since it is current practice that puts the questions, the work opens with a survey of lay services that have sprung up in the last few decades. The action taken by Paul VI is presented in relation to this "explosion of ministries" and in relation to the theology of the laity that preceded the Second Vatican Council, took shape during it, and continued to develop after it.

The second part of the book gives a historical survey of that critical period of church history when lesser ministries of an official kind began to appear alongside the ministries and offices of bishop, presbyter, and deacon. To understand what happened then is to understand the history to which Pope Paul VI made appeal in setting up the offices of acolyte and reader for laymen. Understanding what happened also allows us to gain some insights that are vital to our own future. Along with this survey, the second part of the work reflects on ministry in relation to the ecclesiology of the New Testament.

The interest of the third part of the book is to find a theology that draws on what is presented in the first two parts and to address the question of liturgical ministries more specifically. This theology must explain the place of the laity in the church, the specific character of their mission and ministry, and the process of recognizing and installing ministers.

The difference between the approach to the subject of this book and other books in the series entitled

viii

"Studies in the Reformed Rites of the Catholic Church" is quite obvious. The others have to do with the reforms of rites that are completed, in as much as one can ever use that word of liturgy. Here, we are dealing with a reform scarcely begun. More surmise is therefore inevitable, with regard to the future, and more open comment on present happenings is appropriate.

Since its publication five years ago, the book has apparently been of some use. In any case, the publishers are now ready to go into a second printing, which has provided me with the occasion to make some revisions and to add some features that bring the work up to date. The revisions, however, are not extensive or drastic. Since the work seems to have been helpful in its original form, it seemed best to leave it intact, with only minor revisions made.

David N. Power, O.M.I.
The Catholic University
of America
Washington, D.C.

Monday of the Easter
proclamation of the
holy women, 1985

The Present

Chapter One

Lay Ministry: Documents and Facts of Post-Conciliar Development

Presbyters[1] of an older generation who look back to their seminary days will remember the efforts made to give some importance and solemnity to the reception of tonsure and the four minor orders. They will remember the examinations they had to pass on the matter and form of these orders, as they will remember the lengthy instructions given to subdeacons about washing purificators. These were the externals which served to cover up the fact that men ordained as exorcists would never have to confront the devil or that boys of seven were more often seen in the sanctuary in cotta and cassock than were ordained acolytes.

It was obvious to all who thought about it that when the Roman congregations responsible for worship set about revising liturgical books and rites they would have to do something about the anomalies of tonsure, minor orders and subdeaconate. Occupying as they did a place in the Pontifical, these rites existed only as artificially solemnized steps on the way to the priesthood. What possible place, if any, could be found for such orders in the life and ministry of the church?

In the past, the minor orders and the subdeaconate had taken shape through a curious combination of discipline and clericalization. The discipline affected the lives of candidates for deaconate and presbyterate. Making the minor orders a necessary preparation for these offices assured that the candidates would be subjected to proper scrutiny, particularly in regard to celibacy. The clericalization affected all, for it meant the restriction to clerics of liturgical duties which are not of their nature connected with the clerical state.

These matters were given prominence by several liturgical historians both before and after the Second Vatican Council.[2] The post-conciliar commission charged with the revision of rites had thus to consider two questions. First of all, could the passage through the minor orders be considered necessary or opportune for candidates for the deaconate and priesthood? Secondly, and independently of the answer to the first question, did they have a place and a meaning in the ministry of the church because of their intrinsic nature?

It was not unprovidential that the investigation into minor orders should cross paths with questions about the laity's share in the mission of Christ and his church. That this has its roots in the sacraments of initiation was affirmed by the Council itself. Their role in liturgy certainly expanded rapidly in the aftermath of the Council. At first, however, not much thought seems to have been given to any kind of official designation for the ministerial role of lay persons in the church.

The first decision of the commission which looked into minor orders was to suppress those orders not in any degree exercised by their recipients. These were the orders of exorcist and porter.[3] The commission also decided to retain the offices of lector and acolyte, but stipulated that they should be exercised in pastoral work by those seminarians who received ordination to them. These two offices were deemed a fitting preparation for the priesthood, since they were considered to be a share in it at a lower level.

At this point, the laity entered the picture. While describing service in the sanctuary and the reading of the scriptures in the liturgy as a share in the priesthood of order, the commission nonetheless provided for the exercise of these duties by laity. It saw them as important functions in themselves, and hence as offices to which the local ordinary could formally induct members of the laity when no clerics were available.

MINISTERIA QUAEDAM

When Pope Paul VI eventually made official pronouncement on the issue of minor orders, this was significantly different to what had been originally proposed by the commission. In 1972, this Pope simultaneously issued documents on the minor orders and on the permanent deaconate. These were the *motu proprio, Ministeria quaedam,* and the *motu proprio, Ad pascendum.*[4] Our concern here is with the former rather than with the latter, though it is important to note that the two came together. This shows that the position on lay services is part of an overall restructuring of ministry in the church.

In *Ministeria quaedam,* Paul VI suppressed all use of the word "order" in connection with the ministries formerly designated as minor orders. Of these ministries, he decreed that those of exorcist and porter should be suppressed, at least as general ministries for the whole church, while those of lector and acolyte be retained. In keeping these two ministries, he did not wish them to be in any way reserved to clerics or connected with the clerical state. Nor did he wish them to be viewed as offices conferring a special status on those inducted into them.

These two ministries, the Pope suggests, are important liturgical functions in the life of a Christian community. They are not a share in the priesthood of order, but are exercised by lay people in virtue of their share in the priesthood of Christ through baptism. Because of their importance, they need to be exercised by chosen persons and merit a special installation or institution. This, however, is not to be confused with ordination, which is

5

a name to be reserved for the conferring of episcopacy, presbyterate and deaconate. All of this, the Pope states, is "closer to the truth and more in keeping with the contemporary mind"[5] than were the former canonical and liturgical prescriptions on minor orders. He does, however, maintain one restriction from an earlier tradition, namely, the exclusion of women from these offices.[6]

Ministeria quaedam and *Ad pascendum* do retain something of the sequence of offices or honors in the church, in as much as they prescribe that candidates for the presbyterate must still receive the offices of lector, acolyte, and deaconate prior to presbyterate. Even here, however, the Pope insists that the duties of acolyte and lector are not a participation in the sacrament of order, so that this is not the reason for the law. The reason is rather that the responsibility for the word and the service of the altar which they entail are a good preparation for the greater responsibility of the presbyterate.

The office of lector and that of acolyte are henceforth the only two liturgical offices outside the sacrament of order which have a canonical status and a rite of installation common to all parts of the Latin Church. This does not mean that they are the only liturgical offices to which people can be named and into which they can be inducted by an official blessing. The Pope states "besides the offices common to the Latin Church, there is nothing to prevent episcopal conferences from requesting others of the Apostolic See, if they judge the establishment of such offices in their region to be necessary or very useful."[7] Among such possible offices, he mentions those of porters, exorcists, catechists, and the promotion of works of charity.

As can be readily seen, the Pope followed the suggestions of the commission on several points. He accepted their view that only the offices of acolyte and lector should be retained for the whole Latin Church. He also adopted their suggestion that in the absence of clerics lay persons could be officially installed into these ministries. He differs essentially from the position of the commission in the way that he understands these offices, since he separates them completely from the sacrament of order and from the clerical state. Hence, instead of seeing their conferral on lay persons as an exception he can see this as the normal thing. In other words, he makes it clear that these are lay offices and ministries, not clerical. He also paves the way for an enlargment of the role of the laity in the church in what he says about the possibility of setting up ministries peculiar to the needs of individual churches.

With the document *Ministeria quaedam* in its hands, the Roman Congregation for Divine Worship published the rites of blessing for installation into the ministries of acolyte and lector.[8] The position on lay ministries, however, did not remain stable for long. For reasons known only to those sufficiently acquainted with the intricacies of Vatican administration, another Sacred Congregation also had to have its stake in the matter. In January 1973, the Congregation for the Discipline of Sacraments issued an instruction *Immensae caritatis* on facilitating the distribution and reception of the sacrament of the eucharist.[9] This instruction was in fact a follow-up on a decree, *Fidei custos,* which had been sent to local bishops toward the end of the sixties, about matters related to holy communion.[10]

Among other things, this instruction touched on the question of eucharistic ministry. It laid down that local ordinaries may designate, or permit pastors to designate, some men and women as extraordinary ministers of communion within the confines of their own jurisdiction. These persons are to exercise their ministry by way of complement to that of priests, deacons, acolytes and lectors. The provision for extraordinary ministers is intended to make the distribution of communion easier in large assemblies, to make communion to the sick more common, and to make it possible for all the faithful to receive communion even when ordinary ministers are not available. The persons designated for this ministry may be commissioned by a special church blessing, if the bishops see fit. This new reality has in the future to be taken into account when there is talk of lay participation in the ministry of the church.[11]

WHY SUCH MINISTRIES?

In the documents quoted, these various prescriptions about the functions of the laity in the liturgy are supported by some doctrinal or theological reasons. In *Ministeria quaedam*, Paul VI invokes two principles of the Vatican Council's constitution on the liturgy.[12] The first is the general principle which calls for full and active participation of all the faithful in the church's worship.[13] The second is that which requires an apt distribution of functions and ministries in the assembly.[14] In changing the rules about minor orders and in describing the roles of the acolyte and the lector, the Pope intends to implement these principles. Theologically, therefore, the two ministries are rooted in that priesthood of which the first letter of Peter speaks when it names the Christian people "a chosen race, a royal priesthood, a people set apart" (1 Peter 2.9). In other words, these ministries are a way of realizing the share in Christ's priestly office which the people receive through the sacraments of initiation.

It is apparent from *Ministeria quaedam* that a role in the liturgy involves responsibilities which extend beyond the boundaries of the liturgical assembly. The lector is expected to take some part in the instruction of the faithful who are preparing for the reception of sacraments. He is also expected to be aware of the need to make the Word of God known to non-Christians. On his part, the acolyte is given a supervisory authority over all those

8

who exercise any kind of function in the liturgical assembly.

This extension of responsibilities beyond the assembly may have the implication that a share in one of Christ's three offices involves some particular share in the others. Certainly, it would be a mistake to conclude from *Ministeria quaedam* that Paul VI thought of lay ministry uniquely in terms of liturgy. In his exhortation *Evangelii nuntiandi* of 1975[15] he gives a very broad vision of lay participation in the church's ministries. He endorses the concept that the whole church is missionary and that the laity shares in its mission in virtue of the sacraments of initiation. The point which he emphasizes above all else is the special importance of the Christian laity's presence in the evolution of temporal affairs. This is the usual way in which the gospel can become a leaven in society.

According to *Evangelii nuntiandi*, the development of lay ministries goes along with a movement toward greater community. This is particularly apparent in what are called basic Christian communities. Not only do these represent a greater mutual interest and sharing. They also represent a greater diversification of ministries in the building up of the Christian people. In face of such developments, and just a short space of time after his prescriptions of *Ministeria quaedam*, Paul VI offers the following reflection:

"These ministries, apparently new but closely tied up with the church's living experience down the centuries—such as catechists, directors of prayer and chant, Christians devoted to the service of God's Word or to assisting their brethren in need, the heads of small communities, or other persons charged with the responsibility of apostolic movements—these ministries are valuable for the establishment, life and growth of the church, and for her capacity to influence her surroundings and to reach those who are remote from her."[16]

This reflection puts the norms for the institution of aco-lyte and lector, as well as those for the designation of extraordinary ministers of communion, into proper context. Those norms touch on only one aspect of the laity's involvement in the ministry and mission of the church. They are only a beginning in an official recognition of lay ministry. Certainly, they are not intended to be in the least descriptive of all that has been going on in the church over a period of time.

The practical reasons for naming extraordinary ministers of communion are clearly stated in *Immensae caritatis*. The theological implications are not as clear. In early Christian times, the handling and distribution of the sacred bread was not restricted to the clergy, since to bring communion home for oneself or for the sick was not uncommon.[17] One could therefore argue that this decree is nothing other than a return to such early recognition of the rights of the laity, with new and more contemporary needs in mind. The restriction implied by the need for a special designation could be viewed as due only to the demands of respect and piety among a people not accustomed to such usage.

One cannot, however, be too sure that this is the reasoning behind the decree. *Immensae caritatis* seems firm on the unusual or extraordinary nature of this ministry. The technical term *extraordinary*[18] emphasizes that it is not a matter of course for the laity to handle and distribute the Body and Blood: this is done by them only by way of substitution for official and ordinary ministers. There is, moreover, a special blessing. This gives a certain quality to the ministry which distinguishes it from the common offices of lay persons.

In its own way, therefore, the ruling on extraordinary ministers of eucharistic communion raises questions about differences in role within the laity. Can one distinguish between things which are common to all because of baptism and those which though rooted in bap-

10

tism require special designation? And among these latter, is there a meaningful distinction to be made between those which are given canonical recognition and those which are not?

In 1980, the Sacred Congregation for Sacraments and Divine Worship issued an instruction intended to correct some trends in the celebration of the eucharist that it saw as an abuse.[18a] In the course of this instruction, the congregation seemed to impose a restriction on the liturgical ministry of women. Where the instruction spoke of their ministry, it allowed of their reading the word of God and proclaiming the intentions for the prayer of the faithful, but stated that they could not assume the functions of acolyte or minister at the altar.[18b] What exactly is intended by this prohibition, and how far it can be taken as law, is not clear, but it does betray an unwillingness to give women the same place in liturgical ministry as men, and in this sense is in line with the restrictive mentality of *Ministeria Quaedam.*[18c]

The revised Code of Canon Law, issued in 1983, refers to the liturgical books for liturgical legislation. At the same time, it does state some norms about lay participation in liturgical ministry.[18d] Recalling the possibility of promoting men to the offices of acolyte and reader, it allows for the temporary deputation of any lay person to fulfill the role of reader, commentator, cantor, or other minister necessary to the liturgy as foreseen by law. It also allows that any lay person, when the necessary ministers are wanting and where the needs of the church demand it, may be called upon to exercise the ministry of the work, preside over liturgical worship, confer baptism, and distribute holy communion, in keeping with the prescriptions of law. This but gives formal recognition to the established practice whereby in many countries Sunday services are conducted under the presidency of a

11

lay person, and whereby baptisms are done likewise by lay persons. In the appropriate place, the code also mentions that where ordained ministers are unavailable, lay persons may be delegated to officiate at marriages,[18e] but no mention is made of having lay persons preside at funeral liturgies. There is no exclusion of women from the services mentioned in these canons.

All of this legislation, subsequent to *Ministeria Quaedam*, indicates simply that the document raised the appropriate question of lay liturgical ministry, but that it was too restrictive in its prescriptions to truly meet the church's needs or to take account of what is developing in the lives of the churches around the world.

MINISTRIES IN THE CHURCHES

The development of lay ministries in particular churches did not begin with *Ministeria quaedam* and its provisions. Indeed, one can see the true meaning and import of this papal document only by looking at what had taken place before it and at what continues to develop in various parts of the world. Evidence of this development can be found in positions taken by episcopal conferences and in reports printed in journals and reviews.

One of the episcopacies which has been most expansive in treating the theme of lay ministries is the French. After *Fidei custos*, the French bishops set up norms for the appointment of extraordinary ministers of the eucharist.[19] When the instruction *Immensae caritatis* was published in the wake of *Ministeria quaedam*, the French bishops noted the fact that the country already had extraordinary ministers of the eucharist. They also queried the distinction between acolytes who were to be canonically instituted and extraordinary ministers, who seemed to be given the same function as the acolyte, but without the official name or canonical recognition.[20]

The tone of this response was rather crisp. This is understandable when the matter of ministers for holy communion is seen alongside the much greater reality of lay ministries in the church of France. At their plenary assembly at Lourdes in 1973, the bishops published a document entitled *Tous Responsables dans l'Eglise? Le ministère presbytéral dans l'Eglise toute entière ministèrielle.* [21] It contains reports on what was taking place in the French church and several essays by theologians, including Yves Congar. The position reflected in the booklet is that in a largely dechristianized society, the whole question of ecclesial mission and ministry needs rethinking. The needs of the situation are not met simply by adding official lay ministers to the ordained. What is at stake is a restructuring of ministry and a new understanding of the relation between ordained and lay ministries.

In this restructuring, two facts in particular have to be taken into account, according to the reports here published. The first directly concerns presbyters, the second the laity. The position of the presbyter has become more difficult to sustain. This results not only from a growing dearth of presbyters but also has to do with a kind of crisis of identity in their ranks. Prompted partly by the shortage of presbyters and partly by a greater awareness of their own identity, more and more lay persons were assuming ecclesial responsibilities. This was being done with little fanfare or publicity, but it was of vital significance for the church that it was happening. The reports recall the work done by laity in the Catholic Action Movement, as well as the work done by catechists. They also point to the actual leadership being given by laity in parishes without resident pastors. This leadership includes presiding at Sunday worship in the absence of an ordained presbyter.

The tone of the document indicates that this kind of development has to continue, because both the work of internal renewal and the work of evangelization demand the contribution of the laity, not merely because of the shortage of presbyters. It has to do with the very nature of the church and of its mission in the world. As background to their concern about ministries, the French episcopacy pointed to another report which it had approved at Lourdes in 1971.

This 1971 report was presented to the assembly by Msgr. Robert Coffey and was entitled *Eglise Signe de Salut au Milieu des Hommes*. [22] The immediate occasion for this report seems to have been a concern for proper liturgical development and celebration. From practical concerns about how an assembly should be ordered, Coffey went to the roots of the problem, which he saw as the dechristianization of society and the secularization of the minds of the faithful. His basic position is that without a serious evangelization, the French church could not tackle its problems of prayer and worship. In other words, much church practice had regressed into a kind of ritualism. Even where sacraments continued to be requested and administered, the reality of the church was not evident. The subtitle of the report, *Eglise-Sacrement*, is an appeal to the vision of the church as a sacrament of salvation espoused by the Second Vatican Council. [23] The church has to be defined as a community of faith which gives witness to the salvation offered by God in Jesus Christ. Without faith and without community in faith, there can be no witness and there can be no genuine cult or worship. Hence the need for a program of evangelization.

In such a context, questions about the liturgical ministry of the laity do not appear as the primary concerns of the local church. It is of more fundamental importance that lay people play a part in spreading the gospel and in building up true communities of faith and Christian charity. Since much was already being done in that line, the French bishops took steps at Lourdes to give it approval and recognition and to ask for a restructuring of church ministry which would integrate all roles and responsibilities. Lay liturgical ministries certainly did exist, such as those of presiding at Sunday worship, distributing communion in church and to the sick, reading the scriptures in the assembly, or leading the participation of all who gathered. They were recognized by the bishops as appropriate functions for the laity, but they were seen by them as only a part of a much greater picture.

From France, we can go south to Italy. The major concerns of the Italian episcopacy lie similarly with the problem of evangelization, as witnessed in the report of their general assembly in 1974, *Evangelizzazione e Sacramenti*.[24] They did, however, address themselves more directly than their French brethren to the questions raised by *Ministeria quaedam*. In 1973, the episcopal assembly expressed its intention to make provisions for the offices of acolyte and lector, as well as for the designation of extraordinary ministers of the eucharist.[25] It also took particular note of that section of the papal document which encourages local episcopacies to institute ministries particular to their own churches. While further study of this possibility was encouraged, the provisional suggestions made at the assembly for ministries in Italy pointed to catechists, cantors or psalmists, sacristans and administrators of works of charity. The bishops made specific mention of the need to consider the position of women in the church, both in relation to such ministries and in a more general way.

While making these specific provisions, the Italian bishops backed them up with some ecclesiological considerations on the position of laity in the church. Four doctrinal principles are cited. The first of these is that the nature of the church as a communion is better realized through a variety of ministries. From this, the bishops turn to the definition of the church's sacramen-

15

tality to be found in *Lumen gentium*. They believe that fostering lay ministries gives more body to this reality of a community which manifests Christ's message to the world. Following on this, they evoke a third principle which is that of the complementarity of the "ordained priesthood" and of the "common priesthood" of all the faithful. This is given greater evidence in a variety of lay ministries. Finally, they quote the principle that the liturgy is the source and summit of the life of the church as that principle which justifies special concern for ministries in the assembly.

In pursuing the development of ministries in the intervening years, the Italian church has tried to avoid any dichotomy between liturgy and the other aspects of community life. Unless the liturgy can be seen to reflect a communion in faith and charity, its progress is of little worth. The laity's role in other activities has to be as marked as their role in liturgy. In this context, one rather particular concern of the Italian bishops is that anybody who is given a liturgical office should be known for his greater participation in the building up of the community. This was drawn out at length during the episcopal assembly of 1976 by Bishop Marco Cé.[26] While stressing that official positions on lay ministries were but the explicitation of what is by gospel right the structure of the church, he pointed to the connection which ought to exist between ministry in the assembly and service rendered in the daily life of a community. He applied this particularly to the nomination of lectors and acolytes. Thus he felt that since it is one of the primary tasks of an acolyte to bring communion to the sick, a person appointed to this office ought to be well known for his concern for the sick. Similarly, a person appointed to the office of lector is most appropriately somebody with a good knowledge of the scriptures and anxious to instruct others in them.

This kind of consideration on the offices of acolyte and lector has a twofold interest. First of all, it places the

16

liturgy within the general context of the life of a community. Secondly, it shows that, in the case of each individual, liturgical roles cannot be separated from a more general responsibility for the life of the church.

Turning to positions taken by the German episcopacy, one can see the extent to which questions about lay ministry extend beyond the boundaries of liturgical assemblies. The German Synod of the early seventies had much to say which is of interest on this score, but how the bishops see the matter is more readily apparent from a 1977 statement on the respective roles of presbyter, deacon and lay person.[27]

To understand the statement one has to know something of the German church. Not only is there a shortage of presbyters, but a considerable number of lay people take some theological training and then apply for either part-time or full-time employment in church activities. The result is that there are lay people who occupy pastoral posts of different sorts in the German church. This is the situation that the German bishops wanted to sort out in their statement.

One of their major preoccupations is that laity may come to occupy posts and exercise ministries which are proper to the ordained. This could well seem to imply that what is not given by ordination can be supplied by delegated jurisdiction and official appointment. This would be but a return, in a new way, to the old divorce between the "power of order" and the "power of jurisdiction" which the Second Vatican Council sought to overcome.

To achieve their purpose of distinguishing clearly between the priesthood of the laity and ordained priesthood, the German bishops use two distinct terms to speak of their respective ministries. To ordained ministries they reserve the German word *Amt* and then use *Dienst* for the laity. Both words could actually be used to translate the Greek word *diakonia* of the New Testament, but the bishops obviously wish to give a more formal sound to the former than to the latter and thereby find a way of distinguishing between lay and ordained in the church. Perhaps the sense of the distinction could be rendered in English by translating *Amt* as official ministry or office, and *Dienst* by the more generic word service. The attempt to find a stricter terminology reminds one of the way in which the Second Vatican Council retained the word *ministerium* for the sacrament of order, while using a variety of other words for the service of the laity.

It is not, however, to be concluded that the German bishops wish to discourage lay participation in the service of the gospel and of the church. Like the other episcopacies already quoted, they too repeat the common principle that it is in virtue of their baptism that the laity share in the mission of Christ and of his church. From this it follows that they should be active members of the community and that there is much that they are called upon to do in virtue of their membership of the Christian community. What the bishops want to do is to make clear distinctions between what belongs to the laity and what to the clergy.

To this end, the bishops distinguish between direct service of the church and direct service of the world. While the role of the ordained is in direct service of the church, the laity belong to both camps but have a primary role in the service of the world. In practice this means that whereas the presbyter's primary task is to preach the word, celebrate the sacraments and form Christian community, the lay person's primary task is to give witness to Christ in the service of the world through secular occupations. This is offered both as a theological distinction and as a rule of thumb whereby to sort out questions about the laity's full-time or part-time employment in church activities. As a theological distinction, it allows one to say that all baptized persons who perform their secular duties in a Christian spirit serve the church and the gospel. As a practical rule of thumb, it makes clear what lay persons in church employment should not do and what they can be called upon to do.

When lay persons are given appointments in pastoral work, this should normally be related to the church's presence in the temporal world. It should not be to do presbyteral duties. Occasionally they may be expected to substitute for presbyters or deacons in functions proper to these offices, but this ought not to involve a permanent appointment to this sort of duty. Indeed, when so called upon to substitute for a presbyter or deacon, the lay person is not acting in virtue of his baptismal character but in virtue of a special delegation given by the hierarchy. It is precisely because it involves a separation between order and jurisdiction that the granting of such permanent appointments to lay persons should not become a common practice. It is not specified what these special tasks would be for which a special delegation is necessary, but it is likely that the bishops had in mind such matters as presiding at Sunday services in the absence of presbyter or deacon. From another document of the same conference, it is clear that the bishops include liturgical preaching among the tasks not within the ordinary compass of the lay ministry.[28]

Having made these distinctions, the German bishops then go on to list three kinds of pastoral office to which . the laity may be appointed in virtue of their baptismal priesthood. The first is that of pastoral assistant, attached to a particular community or to a conglomerate of communities. The pastoral assistant's office is to bring the Christian faith to bear on secular concerns. It is exercised in such tasks as teaching catechism, giving religious instruction, or offering personal counseling. The second kind of appointment is that called the office of community assistant. This person is expected to be of direct help to the pastor in the exercise of his ministerial duties, but he is not to assume any of the functions proper to the pastor. By and large, this means helping him to run the parish and performing such duties in the liturgy as it is fitting for a lay person to perform. The third kind of appointment envisaged is that of a person called community helper. His is an administrative charge and his role is to relieve the pastor of the burdens of administration which do not of their nature belong necessarily to the clergy.

This statement of the German episcopacy can be connected with a series of documents concerning the matter of lay preaching in the church of West Germany. The German Pastoral Synod, held over a period of some years, in 1972 passed a declaration which under certain well-defined conditions would warrant bishops commissioning lay persons to preach at the liturgy.[29] This was submitted by the Cardinal of Munich to the Holy See and a reply was received from Cardinal Wright, accepting the proposal in principle, with certain cautions about its implementation. This letter was followed by two documents from the bishops, one in 1973 from the secretary to the episcopal conference and another in 1974 from the conference itself. This laid down the conditions under which the declaration of the Pastoral Synod could be implemented.

Interesting in this sequence of documents is not only the fact itself of lay preaching in the liturgy, but the reasons underpinning its innovation. The Synod had justified its proposal by appealing to the paucity in number of the clergy and to the degree of religious education of the German laity. Its theological reason was in large part borrowed from Yves Congar's argument for Catholic Action. While recognizing that preaching, especially in the liturgy, belongs properly to bishop and presbyter, and that a special commission is needed if a lay person preaches, the Synodal statement suggested that in virtue of the general priesthood of the laity such a delegation would not be unsuitable. The statements of the

Holy See and of the bishops avoid the theological issue, but merely cite the position of the clergy in Germany, the theological culture of many of the laity, and the need for right choice when someone is commissioned.

Reporting at the congress of presidents and secretaries of national liturgical commissions held in Rome in October 1984, Bishop John Cummins gave an account of lay participation in liturgical ministries in the United States of America.[29a] He noted that participation in liturgy was seen by the faithful in the U.S. as a model for participation in the life and ministry of the church on every level. In particular he noted that alongside such ministries as those of reader, psalmist, minister of communion, cantor, and musician, lay persons play an important part in planning Sunday worship and other liturgies. At the same time, Bishop Cummins noted three issues that need to be faced. The first of these is the need to make provision for the liturgical leadership that will have to be assumed by the laity when the decrease in the number of priests catches up with church organization. The other two issues have to do with what appear to be needless restrictions on lay participation in liturgical ministry, the one with the exclusion of women from service of the altar by *Inaestimabile Donum,* and the other with the provision that in the ministering of communion lay persons are only substitutes for priests, not regular ministers on their own account. On this latter score, the bishop pointed to the sign value of always having the laity distribute communion alongside priests and deacons.

This report, given the nature of the meeting at which it was presented, dealt only with liturgical ministry. A long report presented to the bishops of the United States in 1984 on church personnel gives a good account of the general state of ministry in the United States, including the part played in it by lay persons.[29b] First of all, the report remarks on the emergence since the Second Vatican Council of a vast number of ministries that are exercised by lay persons and that pertain both to the inner life and to the mission of the church. Examples given are youth ministry, ministry to the aged, bilingual ministry, ministry to the handicapped, clinical pastoral education, and marriage encounter. Secondly, the report notes that many lay persons are engaged as full-time personnel in the service of either parish or diocese, or in the offices of the Episcopal Conference. The practice of the American church is indeed such that lay persons are appointed to office as diocesan chancellor and parish administrator, and to membership on planning committees of various sorts. In many parishes they serve as directors of liturgy or religious education, as well as directors of specialized ministries, such as ministry to families, the divorced, drug addicts, youth, the aged, and the like. This can involve either a full-time or a part-time engagement as a stable member of church personnel. Summing up the vitality of the church in the United States, the report says:

"It would seem as we look at the restoration of the permanent diaconate, the advances in religious education, the growth of lay volunteers, the increase in new offices of planning and the various other types of ministries and their support systems the data would indicate that neither the numbers serving the church in a special manner nor church services have diminished. The type of personnel, however, has changed. We are going from a high clerical and religious visibility to an integrated visibility of lay persons and ordained permanent deacons with the world of clerics and religious. All things considered, it would seem church vitality is very strong."[29c]

In its conclusions, the report mentions some of the issues now facing the U.S. church. Can this new vital-

22

ity provide for a future when there are fewer priests? What new structures of the church are necessary to fully integrate the developments that have already taken place? What will be the future relation between priests, religious, and laity? Apart from what is presented in this report, it is clear that the resolution or failure to resolve two issues in particular will be of great importance to the future of the church in the United States. The first has to do with the role of women in church ministry and in the exercise of authority and leadership in the church. The second has to do with the procedures followed in choosing and preparing candidates for priestly ordination. Unfortunately, one notes a reactionary trend in recent years that is blocking any serious and open consideration of these two factors of church life. It is to be hoped that the vitality justly noted by the report will be stronger than the forces that seek to stem it.

One of the important elements in the make-up of the U.S. church is the large percentage of Hispanics. The parishes or dioceses with a strong Hispanic presence have their own distinctive approach to the development of church life and ministries, based on the promotion of *comunidades eclesiales de base* within their boundaries and territory.[29d] This brings them closer to developments in Asia, Latin America, and Africa, where ministry is closely related to the growth of grass-roots communities. One of the more interesting and comprehensive publications on ministry is the report of a colloquium sponsored by the Federation of Asian Bishops' Conferences (FABC) in Hong Kong in 1977.[30] The concluding statement of the colloquium speaks in some detail of the ministries peculiar to the needs of Asia. It also points to the basic Christian community as the context most conducive to the development of lay participation and of new ministries. It describes a basic Christian community as follows:

"A group of people is described as a basic community

23

when the number of members is such that they can really know one another, meet with one another, relate to one another. The members are not too far apart to come together frequently. There is a certain degree of permanence among the members. There is also mutual caring, sharing and support. The community strives for common goals and concerns. There is unity and togetherness."[31]

In Asia, as in other poor or oppressed parts of the world, these communities often express their concern for the struggle for justice and relate this to their sense of unity in Christ and to Christian hope. Hence some of the ministries in the community will have specific reference to temporal questions. In Asia, the cultural climate is still highly religious, but Christianity is a minority religion. Dialogue with other religions is therefore important to a Christian people and hence some of its ministries have to do with this. In fact, there are two listings of ministries in the FABC colloquium. One has to do with leadership, the other with ministries in a more general sense.

The first of these listings reads as follows: "Leadership roles in the Christian communities are slowly emerging. Among the more important services and functions that are developing are community leaders, ministers of the eucharist, prayer leader, catechist, treasurer, social worker, youth leader, educator, facilitator or harmonizer of differences, etc."[32]

The other listing includes: evangelist, catechist, ministers for liturgy, ministry of family apostolate, ministry of healing, ministry of interreligious dialogue, ministry of social concern, ministry for youth, ministry to workers, ministry for education, community builders, ministry of communication and ministry of pastoral community leadership.

It is obvious that these two lists overlap in part and that they are not intended to be exhaustive, even when put together. Indeed, the idea that it would be possible to give an exhaustive listing of ministries would be contrary to the outlook of the colloquium. Its intention was to address itself to a developing situation. It tries to give an idea of what is actually taking place and offer some kind of theological reflection on this.

The two lists quoted do show of themselves that the participants in the colloquium did not have a narrow view of what is religious or spiritual. The church cannot move ahead as community in faith unless it is ready to face challenges inherent in economic, social, political and cultural problems. Its concern for these matters has to be reflected in its own ministry. Hence some of the services listed and discussed have to do with the temporal sphere and the church's part in it. This is an integral part of Christian life. In reading the report of this colloquium, one is certainly not listening to a church turned in upon itself.

While addressing themselves specifically to the subject of formal ministry, the participants in the conference did not want to give the impression in their report that Christian service and formal ministry are synonymous or that every Christian has to undertake a specific charge in the community. They support the notion that all the works of a Christian may be done in a spirit of service and favor the building up of a community in love. They also believe that each member can on occasion perform some deeds which are more clearly or formally related to church life and action. At the same time, they make a distinction both theological and terminological between this general notion of Christian service and formal ministry. Hence they write in their concluding statement:

"We term *services* those ways of sharing the church's ministeriality which are undertaken spontaneously and on occasions. These are already in their own manner an expression of the church's service (*diakonia*) and indeed indispensable for the Church's presence in the world. *Ministries* apply more properly to those services which church members undertake with a certain stability and exercise on a sufficiently broad basis, thus sharing formally in the church's responsibility to signify the presence to men of Christ's saving action. All such ministries must be recognized by the community and authenticated by it in the person of its leader."[33]

The paragraph just cited continues by asking for a formal recognition of ministries which involve a measure of permanence. Did it intend that all the ministries listed earlier should be given this recognition? Since the list is long and most of the services mentioned are not of a passing nature, this would mean that installation of lay services would increase considerably. The colloquium did not become more specific on this score. That it did, however, envisage a fairly broad practice of recognition and installation of lay ministers seems to follow from the fact that at one stage it gives a rather spirited defense of the practice against the accusation of undue institutionalization.[34]

No single publication of a scope equal to that quoted from Asia allows us to examine the development of lay ministries in Africa and Latin America. From the evidence, however, which comes from a variety of quarters it is easy to see that in the churches of these continents as well as in those of Asia there is a close connection between basic Christian community and ministry.

Since *Ministeria quaedam* dealt with liturgical ministry, one can first of all note the extent of formal lay liturgical ministries. One paradigmatic example suffices and it is readily documented. It is that of the church in Brazil, from which we have a 1975 report on the exercise of official ministries in the liturgy by laity.[35] The offices listed are those of president of the Sunday assembly, minister of baptism, minister of eucharistic communion, and minister of funeral rites. Though it is not mentioned in this report, we know from another source that the Sacred Congregation for the Discipline of the Sacraments also allows the appointment in Brazil of lay persons to preside at marriage ceremonies as official church witnesses.[36]

This report from one particular country can be immediately related to what we find in the working document distributed to the bishops of the whole Latin American continent, prior to the CELAM conference at Puebla in 1979. This document noted the influence exercised by both *Ministeria quaedam* and *Evangelii nuntiandi* on the exercise of lay ministries in the church.[37] It also mentioned a recent permission granted by the Holy See to Latin American episcopal conferences whereby they could formally install women in new ministries which they themselves would choose to establish.[38]

It seems a matter of no little importance to take note of the perspective from which the Latin American church sees the liturgical ministries of the laity and all forms of official installation to these or other ministries. The working document already quoted from the Puebla conference makes it clear that liturgical ministries are only some of several lay ministries which have received formal approval, since there are other ministries which bear more directly on works of the apostolate. Of all such offices the document notes that they remain specifically lay ministries and that communities need to do their utmost to avoid any clericalization in their regard.

It makes an even more fundamental point when it states that the primary office of the lay person in the service of the church and its mission remains the evangelization of the temporal sphere. In other words, it is chiefly by their work in secular affairs that Christian laity act out their ministerial character as baptized members of Christ.[39] This was in effect the point which received most emphasis in the document which was approved and published at the end of the conference. It certainly did not neglect or ignore the many ministries of direct service to word, liturgy, and community welfare exercised by the laity. On the other hand, it chose to deplore the almost total absence of Christian influence in the public sector, whether it be social improvement, politics, education or cultural expression. It is in this public sector, according to the bishops, that the principal exercise of mission and ministry is required of the laity.[40] It seems all too easy, it notes, for lay persons to become deeply involved in church affairs to the exclusion of temporal concerns. A church which would allow its recognition of lay involvement to take this turn would be making a grave mistake.[41]

In Latin America, the context for a consideration of ministries, as well as for the secular mission of the laity, is the basic Christian community. The emergence and development of this kind of community is rightly associated with Brazil, even though it has now in some form or another sprung up on all continents. The Brazilian conference of bishops followed the phenomenon with care from the beginning but remained publicly tacit on it until 1982, when the conference's permanent council issued a statement entitled "Basic Christian Communities."[41a] Noting the contribution that these communities have made to the strength and mission of the church in Brazil, the council explains the factors inherent in their life that have made of them a positive experience.

If in other countries the term "basic Christian community" seems to be a confused designation of a confused reality, we need not be surprised that even in Brazil it does not have a univocal meaning. Clodovis Boff has noted two distinctive meanings, explaining: "BC's are made up of small groups of an average of ten people; it is most usually a number of these groups—generally ten—grouped in one area, usually a parish, that is known as a BC. A large parish may encompass more than one BC. . . . But the small groups are also sometimes referred to as BC's."[41b]

When the Brazilian bishops in their 1982 document treat of basic Christian communities, they wish to address the entire phenomenon, but they use the title primarily to refer to grouping of groups rather than to the small group. Thus they say that a basic Christian community is formed by families, adults, and youth in a tight interpersonal relationship of faith. These people enjoy solidarity and a common commitment, and together celebrate the word of God and the eucharist. In this way, they can be seen as cells of the greater community, which is the parish or the diocese.

Listing the essential features of basic Christian communities,[41c] the document notes that they are a practical implementation of what the Vatican Council projected when it spoke of the church as the people of God, or as a community in which "to each is given the manifestation of the Spirit for the common good" (1 Cor 12.7). They are furthermore a concrete endeavor to live church life as a sacrament, sign, and instrument of a profound union with God and of the unity of the human race. Within this horizon, the role of the laity is considered in itself, in relation to the sacraments of baptism and confirmation and to the life of the church, rather than as an adjunct to, or participation in, the ministry of ordained priesthood. The document notes that progress has been possible because these communities possess an integral vision of history where the story of humanity and the story of salvation are interconnected, and that it is this integral vision that has led the church of Brazil to commit itself to the quest for justice and to the liberation of the poor, relying upon the vitality of these grassroots communities.

As to the inner force of these cells of the greater church, the bishops point to their cultural integration into the traditions and past of the Brazilian people, and to the way in which the community's entire life is centered upon a unique style of common prayer. This prayer[41d] is fundamentally a listening to the word of God and to the movements of the grace of the Spirit in daily life, especially in the midst of human vulnerability and weakness, where hope is shared. It is a truly common prayer, where every voice is heard, unhindered by class distinctions, whether social or ecclesiastical. It is a prayer in which the poor are present and active, with their traditions of popular religiosity and native religious expression, but lifted up out of any sense of subjection and powerlessness by the awareness of the action of the Spirit in their own lives and by the knowledge of Christ.

The description of the community, its commitment and its prayer, is very important because it provides the context within which the bishops see the growth of ministries taking place. Affiliation into a basic Christian community means initiation into the communion of prayer and reflection, where discernment takes place. Any decisions affecting the life of the community, and any personal initiatives of ministry, are rooted in the life of the community and are taken in an action of discernment that follows the model of common prayer. Hence, it is in this communion of faith that one finds the seeds of charism and ministry. The call of the Spirit is born in the community; ministries are exercised by members of the community and for the community. Whatever training in faith and ministerial competency is needed for individual members is undertaken as a responsibility of the community. The relation of any minister to the community comes from the fact that the call has been born and discerned, as well as recognized, within its womb. This includes a whole range of ministries, including those of leadership in the various tasks necessary to growth, such as worship, study of the word, social action, community welfare, health care, the struggle for justice, and the like. There is no dichotomy between the holy and the secular, because the community's life is open to the growth of the human within the grace of God's presence and action, and to the discernment of the Spirit in all human activities. There is no sense in which it can be felt that those who lead through a ministry of worship have a different set of concerns from those who are inspired by the life of common faith and sharing to take up the practical tasks of health care, cooperative, or credit union in the wider human community. The life of the church can develop only within the greater human society, and in the service of those who struggle within it to find human dignity and meet human need.

The kind of growth in ministry that takes place through a discernment rooted in common life is well described by Enrique Dussel:

"In a very different way from that prevailing in charismatic movements or religious communities, the basic communities (through their social composition, and their links with the institutional hierarchy, especially in Brazil) possess a charismatic calling devoid of enthusiasms, tongues and extraordinary apparitions, one embedded in the normal daily round of Christian existence and carrying out a deep renewal without making a great deal of noise about it. The 'life revision' (a new version of 'discernment of spirits'), faith or mutual confidence in the members of the community and all services are lived in charity and hope. These base communities today provide the closest analogy with the communities to which Paul wrote: they generate apostles and evangelists whom they send out to start other communities; they produce their own pastors and masters and their own prophets. Their institutionalized ministry is harmoniously linked to the powers of those members who act on the strength of their own charismatic responsibility."[42]

Since I have mentioned basic Christian communities both in Asia and in Latin America (and one would have to do the same in speaking of Africa), it is well to note some ambiguity which surrounds the use of the term. It is in fact a rather misleading translation from the Romance languages and might more correctly read "grass-roots community." The sense of the expression is that this is a community whose faith development begins with the baptized and their gifts, and whose ministerial structuring is founded on that basis.

Historically, the movement associated with this type of community owes more to Brazil than to any other country. It has so happened that other churches were inspired by this movement and so have taken it as a pastoral model of development, adopting at the same time the term basic Christian community. However, once the initiative comes from the ordained pastors rather than from the laity or from the community as a whole the movement does begin to diverge from the original. It might then in some cases be better simply to talk of small Christian communities, realizing certainly that they often derive inspiration from the more original basic community.

To get a more graphic idea of how such communities and their lay ministries actually evolve, it is useful to take one example. Progress is well-documented by a report on the three general assemblies of the Mindanao-Sulu Pastoral Conference (Philippines) that began in 1971.[43]

A joint pastoral letter of the Bishops of Mindanao-Sulu convoking the first pastoral conference for November

1971 shows a fairly self-conscious beginning to what was devised as a movement of church renewal:

"It is with a strong sense of urgency and concern that we feel we must come together to see what we can and must do to renew ourselves as a people, and more specifically, as a Christian people . . . we must work out the directions we should take now if we are to be responsive to the needs of the nation as a whole and of the Church Universal as well. Hence in the spirit of the times, we must examine ourselves and ask some hard questions about ourselves as Christian Community, about our responsibilities in community, about our part in the integral human development of our people—again, as Community.

"More in particular: What new structures must be set up in the Church of Mindanao-Sulu to meet modern demands? What should be the roles of clergy, religious, laity in those new structures?"[44]

Some of the reports to the second pastoral conference, held in 1974, show what was accomplished in a relatively short time, as well as some of the problems of growth experienced. Communities were made small, centered in the local barrio or village rather than in the older parish church which served a wider region. They were conceived, and to a great extent functioned, as total communities, built on faith and taking in every aspect of life, since the gospel was thought to bear on all questions without exception. Lay leadership was exercised in organizing education seminars for justice, nutrition programs, education for responsible parenthood, farmers' organizations and cooperatives, relief programs and rehabilitation programs. Laity, men and women, also assumed roles in worship, "distributing communion, preaching, invoking God's blessing on things, and baptizing, etc."[45] In practice, this meant regular Sunday assemblies and celebration of baptism or funerals presided over by lay ministers. Lay persons, in other words, looked after the ordinary routine of community life, encouraged and helped by the occasional visit of a presbyter and by education seminars directed to leaders.

After several years of such practices, a number of problems were outlined at the second pastoral conference of the region. These were not, indeed, seen as obstacles to growth but rather as indications of where growth could go. It was pointed out, for example, that since laity often assumed liturgical roles that would normally be taken by clergy, this was sometimes taken to be the only development of lay participation in the church. The conference, however, "also recognized that even if there were an abundance of presbyters the laity still have their share in the priesthood of Christ."[46] The conference saw that the situation raises the question of ordination as much as it raises the question of lay ministry. Perhaps it would be necessary eventually to change the discipline surrounding ordination to the presbyterate, as well as the life-style of the ordained minister, in order to meet the needs and the cultural situation of the Mindanao-Sulu church. In the meantime, however, some satisfaction with the current situation was felt, since it provided the opportunity "to encourage the team approach, core groups of lay leaders developing their own style and exercising real authority and responsibility over some areas of community life."[47]

The relation of the lay leader to the community was also seen as an important question. The tendency was noted whereby pastors at times picked those whom they themselves thought suitable. In face of this, it was recommended that "these persons emerge from their own people, thereby promoting the growth of both the leaders and the community where they come from."[48] Along with this went the recommendation that education ought not to focus too much on the leaders. On the contrary, it ought primarily be directed to the community, since it would only be out of community consciousness that the proper choice of leaders could take place.[49] This could be paraphrased by saying that the development of the sense of lay participation in the mission of Christ and in responsibility for community is the only context in which special ministries, both lay and ordained, can suitably emerge.

By the time the Mindanao-Sulu Pastoral Conference held its third assembly in 1977, the issues were no longer those of community leadership or organization. The members of the assembly were then more concerned about the relation of church to culture, about social and political problems, and about the continuing Christian–Muslim tension in the southern Philippines.[50]

One final observation seems worth making about this development of a particular church. The pastoral leaders of this church were to some extent men in a hurry. They saw the urgency of facing up to serious social, political and liturgical questions. Fired by their own enthusiasm, they looked to the basic community program of the Latin American church as a model and sought to implement this. But after a few years, they could see that the movement was still very clerical, that the presbyters in charge could be accused of some manipulation and that though laity were often active in their programs, the church was still subject to clerical rule and direction. None of this, however, had to be regretted. Important steps had been taken, but the necessary process of self-examination could now modify the direction taken. At this stage, it seems that the church in Mindanao is really ready to be more community centered and to allow the laity a greater voice and greater responsibility. What happens next may not be what the clergy want, but what a more conscious laity is led to bring into operation. The bishops of the region do not hesitate to see in all of this the work of the Spirit, while at the same time they recognize that the most important question about ministries is the question about the existence and functioning of a Christian community as a whole. At the same time, in the 1980s they are pursuing a pastoral policy of education in the faith that follows the model of group gatherings, local and regional, and of community participation. They see that it is necessary for the church of the region and for local communities to see how far their options and their actions are dictated by inspirations of faith, and indeed to develop a fuller knowledge of the teachings of the faith.

The growth of community responsibility and the emergence of fresh lay ministries in the churches of Asia, Africa and Latin America is truly massive and one can give only rather summary data here. It is, however, enough to present the picture and to allow one to draw some conclusions.

Several factors contribute to what is happening. There is first the pragmatic need to provide for a grave shortage of presbyters, if the faithful are to continue to have benefit of community, sacraments, pastoral care and teaching. Coupled with the inspiration of the teachings of the Second Vatican Council, this has produced a movement to commit more authority and responsibility to lay persons, both women and men. This in turn makes new style communities an imperative, so that the development of ministries becomes part and parcel of collegial communities. While some first tentatives are more focused on worship than on anything else, time seems to indicate that worship can only be true worship if it is part of a more broadly based community life. Hence the community under its lay leadership looks to matters of the temporal order, inclusive of mutual care within the community and of its responsibility in the social, political and cultural arena. All of this is explained in terms of a theology which sees charism and Spirit as vital forces in church life and mission.

Naturally, there are some things to question in what is happening. Because the whole movement is linked with a shortage of presbyters, there is inevitably ambiguity or risk inherent in it. Some lay persons, men and women, are clearly taking on roles which substitute for ordained ministers, when no candidate for ordination can be found who meets the present discipline and official persuasion that the presbyterate has to be male, celibate and permanent. Were there the kind of change envisioned by many, some of these lay ministries would revert to ordained ministers, often through the simple process of ordaining the present incumbents.

Along with this ambiguity, there goes the risk that the assumption of responsibility by laity could be exhausted in such endeavors, thus beclouding the real nature of lay priesthood and lay ministry. As the Puebla conference of bishops pointed out, it is necessary to think of lay mission in terms of the temporal order. Whether or not one accepts the division which gives the presbyter responsibility for pastoral care and liturgy and the lay person responsibility for the temporal order, it is clear enough that the greater lay consciousness which we now witness ought indeed be the occasion to think about the church's role in the entire human orbit and about ministries which look to this. This is the really basic question about ecclesial ministry: how does a church community evangelize the human community, and what shape do ministries take when this is its concern. We can be grateful that our sister continents have shown how much this is a community question, and that all questions about ministry must now take this as their living context.

CONCLUSIONS
It is time to conclude the survey of position and fact which this chapter set out to give. Among the host of papal and other magisterial documents of the last fifteen years, *Ministeria quaedam* at first pales into insignificance

and the rites for the installation of acolyte and lector are truly a tailpiece to the rites of the Roman Church, with but little impact on anything that goes on in churches. It may, however, be a case of "the mouse that roared." What these documents on ministry have done is not measurable by their content. It is the extent to which they help us to focus our attention on the truly vast, complex and rich reality of lay mission and ministry in the church that they take their place within the process of ecclesial renewal.

Clearly, the realities of lay responsibility and lay service go far beyond the few ministries mentioned in *Ministeria quaedam* and *Evangelii nuntiandi*, as they go beyond the boundaries of the liturgical assembly. Even though Paul VI and official positions generally tend to treat of liturgical ministry as something male, the facts of the matter indicate that women are prominent in lay ministries, especially in the Third World. Consequently, the theology of ministry, inclusive as it must be of both order and lay roles, has to speak to the issue of women in the church. The very tendency for the liturgical and the temporal to compenetrate also shows that the fundamental principles of a theology of ministry will have to do with the mission of the church in the world.

Whatever the indecisions and ambiguities, the church is working out the implications of the Vatican Council's teaching on the laity and is trying to do this in conjunction with the facts of church life rather than in a purely abstract manner. Thus, the ecclesiological principle which states the call of the laity to share in the mission and ministry of the church on the basis of their share in Christ's own ministry, is everywhere accepted. It is within this context, and not in opposition to it, that problems about the relation between ordained and lay, about the place of women, and about such things as the meaning of installation rites have been stated. The extent, however, to which these concerns postulate a new ecclesial structure is not often found in statements. It is more the lived experience that calls this to our attention.

NOTES

1. In keeping with the usage of this series, the word *presbyter* is used in this book as the English equivalent of the Greek and Latin *presbyter*. Hence it designates the holder of the second rank among the ordained. Where *priest* or *priesthood* is used of the clergy, it refers to their liturgical functions.

2. W. Croce, "Die niederen Weihen und ihre hierarchische Wertung," *Zeitschrift für katholische Theologie* 70 (1948) 257-314; B. Botte, "Le Problème des Ordres Mineurs," *Questions Liturgiques et Paroissiales* 46 (1965) 26-31; J. Lécuyer, "Les Ordres Mineurs en Question," *La Maison-Dieu* 102 (1965) 26-31.

3. See R. Béraudy, "Les Ministères Institués dans 'Ministeria quaedam' et 'Ad pascendum,'" *La Maison-Dieu* 115 (1973) 86-96.

4. English text: *The Rites of the Catholic Church as Revised by Decree of the Second Vatican Ecumenical Council and Published by Authority of Pope Paul VI* (Pueblo Publishing Co., New York 1976) 732-739, 726-731.

5. *The Rites* 728.

6. *The Rites* 730.

6. *The Rites* 730.

7. *The Rites* 728.

8. *The Rites* 740-745.

9. English text: *Vatican Council II: The Conciliar and Post-Conciliar Documents*, Austin Flannery, O. P., ed. (Costello Publishing Co., Northport, New York 1977) 225-232.

10. The text was never made public. A French translation may be found in *Documentation Catholique* 67 (1970) 310-316. For a commentary, see J. Didier, "Le Ministre Extraordinaire de la

Distribution de la Communion," *La Maison-Dieu* 103 (1970) 73-85.

11. For a commentary, see *Notitiae* 9 (1973) 168-173.

12. *The Rites* 727.

13. *Sacrosanctum Concilium* 14: Flannery 7-8.

14. *SC* 28: Flannery 11.

15. Paul VI, *Evangelii nuntiandi*. English translation: *On Evangelization in the Modern World* (USCC, Washington, D.C. 1976).

16. Op. cit., n. 73.

17. See Didier, art. cit.

18. The Latin term *extraordinarius* is translated as "special" in the latest documents published by the International Committee for English in the Liturgy. Thus, lay ministers of the eucharist are now called "special ministers" rather than "extraordinary ministers." I prefer to retain "extraordinary."

18a. Sacred Congregation for the Sacraments and Divine Worship, "Inaestimable Donum," AAS 72 (1980) 331–343.

18b. l.c. 338.

18c. For a discussion of its binding force in canonical perspective, cf. John M. Huels, "Female Altar Servers: The Legal Issue," *Worship* 57 (1983) 513–525.

18d. Code of Canon Law, canon 230.

18e. Canon 1112, par. 1.

19. "Note de la Commission Episcopale Française de la Liturgie," *Documentation Catholique* 67 (1970) 311-317.

20. *Documentation Catholique* 70 (1973) 361.

21. *Assemblée Plénière de l'Episcopat Français, Lourdes 1973, Tous Responsables dans l'Eglise?* (Le Centurion, Paris 1973).

22. Robert Coffy and Roger Varro, *Eglise Signe de Salut au Milieu des Hommes: Eglise-Sacrement: Rapports Présentés à l'Assemblée Plénière de l'Episcopat Français, Lourdes 1971* (Le Centurion, Paris 1972).

23. *Lumen gentium* 1.

24. "Evangelizzazione e Sacramenti: Documento Pastorale dei Vescovi Italiani," *Il Regno: Documentazione* XVIII (1973) 396-405.

25. Conferenza Episcopale Italiana, "I Ministeri nella Chiesa. Documento Pastorale," *Notiziario CEI* 8 (1973) 157-168.

26. Marco Cé, "Ministeri Istituiti e Ministeri Straordinari," *Il Regno: Documentazione* 21 (1976) 266-271.

27. *Wiener Dioezesan Blatt*, April 1977. French translation: *Documentation Catholique* 74 (1977) 517-522.

28. Conférence Episcopale Allemande, "La Participation des Laics à la Prédication en Allemagne Fédérale," *Documentation Catholique* 71 (1974) 645-646.

29. Communiqué du Rapporteur de la Conférence Episcopale Allemande, "Les Prédicateurs Laics," *Documentation Catholique* 70 (1973) 1081.

29a. Bishop John Cummins, "Report at Congress of Presidents and Secretaries of National Liturgical Commissions, October 23–28, 1984," *Origins* 14 (1984) 400–405.

29b. Eugene Hemrick, "Report on Church Personnel: Developments in Ministry," *Origins* 13 (1984) 561–566. See also the letter of the U.S. bishops on the laity, *Origins* 10 (1980) 369–373.

29c. l.c. 564.

29d. Cf. "U.S. Bishops' Pastoral Letter on Hispanic Ministry," *Origins* 13 (1984) 529–541.

30. The concluding statement of the colloquium was published as "Asian Colloquium on Ministries: Conclusions," *Origins* 8 (1978) 129-143.

31. Loc. cit., 135.

32. Ibid., 136.

33. Ibid., 133-134.

34. Ibid., 134.

35. "Brasilia: Relatório sobre os Ministérios Litúrgicos Exercidos por Leigos," *Notitiae* 11 (1975) 263-268.

36. Sacred Congregation for the Discipline of the Sacraments, "Instruction Empowering Lay Persons to Preside at Marriages in Brazil, 15 May, 1974," *Doctrine and Life* 25 (1975) 670-672.

37. *III Conferencia General del Episcopado Latinoamericano: La Evangelizacion en el Presente y en el Futuro de America Latina. Documento de Trabajo,* mimeographed, par. 266.

38. Ibid., n. 5 "Los Ministerios en la Iglesia," par. 6: "La reforma de la disciplina de la antiguas ordenes minores . . . la riqueza del enfoque dado por la 'Evangelii nuntiandi' a estos servicios eclesiales y la reciente facultad de otorgar a mujeres los nuevos ministerios que las Conferencias episcopales establezcan, constituyen puntos muyo importantes en la conciencia y la prática de la Iglesia de hoy."

39. Ibid., par. 243.

40. *III General Conference of Latin American Bishops: Evangelization at Present and in the Future of Latin America: Conclusions,* Official English Edition (National Conference of Catholic Bishops, Washington, D.C. 1979), par. 787: "The fact is that lay people, by virtue of their vocation, are situated in the Church and in the world. Members of the Church, loyal to Christ, they are pledged to the construction of the Kingdom in its temporal dimension." See par. 789-795.

41. Ibid., par. 823-825.

41a. Conselho Permanente de CNBB, "Comunidades Ecclesiais de Base," *Comunicado Mensal: Conferência Nacional dos Bispos de Brasil,* Novembre de 1982, no. 362, 1180–1195.

41b. Clodovis Boff, "The Nature of Basic Christian Communities," *Concilium* 144, 53. On the significance of basic Christian communities, cf. Leonardo Boff, *Church: Charism and Power. Liberation Theology and the Institutional Church,* translated by John W. Diercksmeier (Crossroad, New York 1985) 125–130, 131–137, 154–164.

41c. l.c. no. 12, 1181f. See the section III "A CEB e los pobres."

41d. For a fuller description of this prayer, cf. Inaĉio Neutzling, "Célébrations dans les Communautés de Base," *Spiritus* XXIV (1983) 115–125.

42. E. Dussel, "The Differentiation of Charisms," *Charisms in the Church*, C. Floristan and C. Duquoc, eds., *Concilium* 109, 51.

43. M. Gaspar, *What is the Mindanao-Sulu Pastoral Conference*, no date or place. A report on ministries in Africa, Asia, Europe and Latin America can be found in *Pro Mundi Vita*, no. 62, September 1976.

44. Gaspar 47.

45. Ibid., 30.

46. Ibid.

47. Ibid., 31.

48. Ibid.

49. Ibid.

50. Ibid., 36-39.

Chapter Two

Practice in Search of a Theology

Pope Paul's decisions on lay ministries, and all the other positions taken by episcopal conferences or other bodies on these questions, were intended to be an implementation of the principles of the Second Vatican Council. These principles came from its doctrinal presentation of the mystery of the church, and to understand this it is necessary to go back to the two decades which preceded the Council.

BEFORE THE COUNCIL

With roots in such works as E. Mersch's *Theology of the Mystical Body*[1] and with some measured encouragement as well as caution from the encyclical *Mystici corporis*,[2] some theologians in the aftermath of World War II began to publish an ecclesiology which took the laity's mission into account. This ecclesiology had the advantage that it took practical truth into consideration, as well as doctrinal tradition. It related to the success of the liturgical movement in developing a greater lay participation in divine worship, and to the role in society of the Catholic Action movement. The laity, long left out of treatises on the church except under the title of subject, were acknowledged in practice to have an active part in worship as well as in apostolate in the temporal world. How could a theology of the church, it was asked, account for this active role?

Writings on the liturgy, within the context of the liturgical movement, had already offered some explanation of lay participation in worship. This was done by speaking of the lay person's relation to the priesthood of Jesus Christ. Through baptism and confirmation, the Christian is given the grace to live in obedience to the gospel and in the service of others. This is to offer a spiritual sacrifice, pleasing to God, and it is the principal way in which the baptized Christian shares in the priesthood of Jesus Christ. These two sacraments, however, also confer a sacramental character, in virtue of which the Christian actively shares in the public worship of the church, thereby joining the offering of a holy life to the offering of Jesus Christ which is represented in the eucharist and active in the other parts of the liturgy as source of worship and of grace.

In this way, the theology of worship had expanded on the teaching of Aquinas about the sacramental character. Aquinas explained that the sacramental character was a configuration to Christ the Priest, which allowed for the church's union with him in offering praise and sacrifice to God and in sanctifying humankind.[3] The character conferred through the sacrament of order, in his explanation, was an active character or power, allowing the priest to act in the name of Christ. The character conferred through baptism he described as a passive power, which made it possible for the Christian to receive the other sacraments. The neatness of his schema, however, was somewhat broken by the need to explain the character given at confirmation. Here, instead of relating it to public worship, he explained that it was a power to profess the Christian faith publicly.[4]

In the context of the liturgical movement, writers used this explanation while adapting it. The principal adaptation had to do with the baptismal character, which they were not satisfied to explain as a passive power related only to the reception of sacraments. On the contrary, since it was indeed a configuration to Christ the Priest, it could be explained as the root of an active participation in the offering of the eucharistic sacrifice and in all the other actions of the church's public worship. This explanation was, in the main, accepted by Pope Pius XII in his encyclical *Mediator dei*. Here he taught that the laity offer the Mass in union with the priest by reason of their own particular share in Christ's priesthood, which comes to them through baptism.[5] Despite an admonitory tone cautioning against too wide an application of this principle, the document as a whole was looked upon as a moment of gain for the liturgical movement. Today, there may seem nothing remarkable in the statement, but after centuries of lay passivity in the liturgy it was no mean advance.

But, it was apparent that it was not enough for ecclesiology to speak of lay participation in worship. The considerable apostolic work of the members of Catholic Action in its various forms had also to be taken into account. The church's mission to make Christ's gospel known and effective in the world could not be achieved without the commitment and action of the laity. But if one simply ascribes this to the call which comes with baptism, what has then to be said about all those who seek to live good lives but do not engage in any formal apostolate? Or what has to be said about the standard theology of the church, which attributed mission and apostolate in principle to the hierarchy? Developing new trends in ecclesiology to a great extent meant working out an answer to this twofold tension which arose from Catholic Action. On the one hand, how could Catholic Action be related to the common vocation of the lay person; on the other how could it be related to the mission given by Christ to the hierarchy?

Catholic Action was militantly apostolic, with its branches for workers and for students, and with its particular focus on youth in both cases. One cannot generalize too much about Catholic Action by comparing countries such as Belgium, France and Italy, for in each of these it had its own particular physiognomy. However, it can be said that by and large its concern was the loss of the world to the church, whether in the form of the working masses or in the form of political and secular institutions.

It was the consequent feeling that the laity were in effect involved in a work of re-Christianization which explains how the movement provoked theologians to revise their theories and examine Christian doctrine. It is helpful to contrast the European scene with that in the United States in order the better to understand the theological currents which influenced the teaching of the Vatican Council. In America, there were certainly lay persons deeply involved in living out their Christian vocation in the service of others, but they did not face the question of de-Christianization. Their apostolate was largely the social apostolate, the care of the needy and distressed of society. Their social concern rendered them naked to the accusation of "going communist," but they could not easily be accused of taking over the church's teaching office. In Europe, or at least in France and Belgium, on the contrary, what prompted the laity's concern was the loss of faith among workers and among youth generally, and the loss of Christian sense in the running of secular affairs. Hence, they took on a task of evangelization, a task not only of implementing the gospel on the social scene, but one of making the gospel known.

Yves de Montcheuil was one of the first theologians to address himself to this question.[6] He worked out a theology of vocation which stated that every Christian had an apostolic calling by the very fact of being a member of the church. He defined this as the call to give witness to Christ in the midst of the world. Catholic Action has to be founded on this, but it is not the only way of living out one's call and is not necessary for all. This was to state the general principle of the apostolic nature of the Christian call and to provide the context within which Catholic Action could be further explained. It is interesting to note the emphasis given to this principle by Pius XII a decade later in his address to the 1957 world congress for the lay apostolate.[7]

It remained to be explained how Catholic Action and its type of evangelization could be described as a distinctively lay apostolate, without violating the principle that Christ's mission had been confided through the Twelve to the hierarchy. The principal author to deal with this question was Yves Congar, in his justly famous *Jalons pour une Théologie du Laicat*.[8] This was a comprehensive treatment of the lay person's call, within which compass special attention was given to the questions raised by Catholic Action.

As Congar then explained it, the most fundamental thing about being a Christian is to share in the sacrifice of Jesus Christ by the spiritual sacrifice of a holy life and by every good deed which leads to communion with God.[9] This is how we are called to live in the time between the sacrifice of Christ on the cross and the consummation of this mystery in his second coming. It is to this fundamental vision that we are to relate the cult and the apostolate of the church. All are called to share actively in cult by the sacramental character, whether that of order or that of baptism and confirmation, but of course in different ways. All are likewise called to the apostolate through the sacraments of order and of initiation, but again in different ways.

The primary way in which the baptized participate in the apostolate, according to Congar, is by prayer and the witness of a Christian life. To explain how Catholic Action in its own particular way is a share in the apostolate, Congar appealed to the double source or origin of the church's mission, namely, the sending of the apostles and the sending of the Holy Spirit, both of which come from Christ. As an institution possessing a mission and the powers to execute it, the church relates back to the twelve apostles. As a community of life, giving witness to Christ in the world and serving others in charity, it originates in the Holy Spirit. The apostolate of the laity has its source in the mission of the Spirit, not in that of the apostles, and its general character is to bring about the consecration of the world through involvement in secular affairs in a Christian spirit and following Christian principles. What happens in Catholic Action is that the mission which the laity receive from the Spirit is taken up under the direction of the hierarchy and ordered toward a specific objective which is that of evangelization. In this way, it becomes also a share in the mission of the hierarchy, even while remaining rooted in the sacraments of initiation and being a way of carrying out the distinctively lay calling of the *consecratio mundi*. Laity do not need any new consecration in order to undertake this apostolate, since they are fitted to it by baptism and the grace of the Spirit. All that is needed to make it a share in the church's mission is a mandate from the hierarchy.

It is of interest to draw attention to Congar's *excursus* on minor orders in the *Jalons*.[10] He refers there to several studies which had pointed out that the minor orders were not originally intended to be steps toward the presbyterate. They were a liturgical consecration of persons who intended to devote themselves in a permanent way to the service of the church, through the exercise of specific functions designated by the title of each of the orders. In view of this history, it had been suggested that minor orders be revised as a consecration of those who devoted themselves in new ways to the permanent service of the church's mission, as, for example, in lay religious congregations.

Congar objects strongly to the idea that lay persons need a special liturgical consecration in order to take on a specific or permanent apostolic task, which does not of its nature belong to the sacrament of order. By baptism, he contends, they are already fitted to serving by their lives, and all that they need beyond this in order to assume a specific apostolate of teaching or evangelization, even in a permanent way, is a mandate from the hierarchy. To require a liturgical blessing for this apostolate would be to deny its lay status and clericalize its service.

On the other hand, Congar did at the time continue to look upon liturgical ministries of the type associated with the minor orders as properly clerical and not lay. He did not have any problem about laity occasionally performing liturgical ministries, since history showed that they could even minister baptism and anointing, but he did see a permanent ordering to liturgical service or ministry as something which had to be seen as clerical and a share in the functions of the hierarchical priesthood. He did therefore think that it was quite fitting that laity, who permanently replaced clerics in the functions of acolyte, reader or porter, should receive the minor orders. This, he believed, was a position advocated by the Council of Trent but not pursued after it.

In view of what I shall later discuss, it is interesting to note one or two things about Congar's position. In the first place, the way that he then thought of all liturgical blessing as a kind of special consecration which smacked of clericalism contrasts with the arguments put forward by Paul VI that such a blessing is only the due recognition by the church of what is properly a lay office. Secondly, whereas today the discussion is about how far the liturgical ministry of the laity extends, for Congar at the time he wrote, all liturgical service, undertaken in a permanent way, pertained to clerical office. Thirdly, Congar said that because of baptismal consecration, a hierarchical mandate is all that is necessary to allow laity to take part in the apostolate. Today, however, many people think that to insist on a hierarchical mandate is to put limits on the laity's part in the church's mission.

Congar's book certainly did not solve once and for all the question about the distinction of cleric and lay person. Much of the writing on the subject emphasized the laity's secular involvement, and used the epithet *secular* as the key to the distinction between hierarchy and laity. Anything that could be seen as a direct way of making Christ present in the secular arena could be considered a lay function. This was, however, a kind of two-edged sword which in some cases put more limits on the laity's role than did Congar, even while accounting in a positive way for the ground of their apostolic mission. In one of his articles, Karl Rahner suggested that whenever lay persons perform either a teaching or a liturgical function they step outside their identity as lay persons and take on what is properly a clerical function.[11]

Speaking to the congress on lay apostolate, Pius XII gave what was considered by many to be an answer to Rahner, by employing the scholastic distinction between order and jurisdiction. The essence of the clerical status, he said, is to be found in order or priesthood, not in jurisdiction or in teaching. When, therefore, a lay person is called upon to teach religion or give catechesis, this is a form of collaboration with the hierarchy which is quite appropriate to lay status and vocation.[12] While this gave a more positive view of the laity's share in the teaching mission of the church, it did not address itself to their liturgical ministry, but left the position as stated in *Mediator dei*. Nor did it address Rahner's problem about separating order and jurisdiction.

The influence of Yves Congar on the positions taken by the Second Vatican Council on ecclesiology and on the laity in the church was incontestably great. The Constitution on the Church and subsequent documents explained the laity's part in the life and mission of the church through reference to the priestly, prophetic and royal office. With regard to single issues, to be detailed shortly, they followed Congar in explaining the relation between hierarchy and laity, using as he did the secular characteristic of the lay office on the one hand and their baptismal consecration on the other. One of the great things the Council did was to place the church and its mission in the world in a new perspective, and in so doing made it possible to approach the laity–clergy problem, as well as many others, from a new angle. Congar himself was able to say in 1965 that Vatican II had introduced a new equilibrium into ecclesiology, whose consequences had not been drawn out by the Council itself and which it would take considerable time to reckon both in theory and in practice.[13]

SECOND VATICAN COUNCIL
As has often been repeated, the truly singular thing about the teaching of the Second Vatican Council is the self-image of the church adopted by the Constitution on the Church. The image of the People of God which prevails today has far-reaching effects on the way in which the respective missions of clerics and laity are conceived and lived. According to this way of looking at the church, it is the church as God's People which receives and bears Christ's mission and is his sacrament in the world. The primary mission is not that given to the hierarchy, nor can we distinguish between the mission of the apostles and the mission of the Spirit. Christ's mission and Spirit are given to the body of the church, so that laity and clergy share in their respective ways in the one mission of God's People and in the triple office of Jesus Christ as Priest, Prophet and King. While the Council constantly related the mission of the laity as well as the mission of the hierarchy to this one source and finality, it is true that it did not completely overcome ambiguity in the way that it distinguished between laity and clergy.

In working out the distinct roles of presbyter and lay person, the Council relied to a great extent on the distinction between immediate or direct service of the church community, and service of the church's role in the secular arena. This is stated as a kind of working principle in *Lumen gentium*, no. 31, where typological definitions of cleric, religious, and lay person are offered:

"Their secular character is proper and peculiar to the laity. Although those in Holy Orders may sometimes be engaged in secular activities, or even practice a secular profession, yet by reason of their particular vocation, they are principally and expressly ordained to the sacred ministry. . . . But by reason of their special vocation it belongs to the laity to seek the kingdom of God by engaging in temporal affairs and directing them according to God's will."[14]

Following up on this typology, this chapter of the Constitution relates the laity's share in the priestly, royal, and prophetic office primarily to their place in secular life. It is by the spiritual offering of their lives that they share in Christ's priesthood, by the witness of their Christian presence that they represent him as prophet, and by the serving of the world in the Spirit of Christ and according to the teachings of the gospel that they submit the world itself to his kingdom. The chapter does, however, show that there are also more special ways in which laity can participate in the church's work and mission, whether in the direct service of Christian communities or in the task of evangelization. Thus no. 33 talks of ministries which constitute a special cooperation or association with the hierarchy, as well as of appointment by the hierarchy "to some ecclesiastical offices with a view to a spiritual end." There is a reference within the paragraph to the men and women who helped Paul in his missionary labors, and the footnote refers to the talk of Pius XII to the lay congress of 1957. Without, therefore, spelling out the details, the Council here recognizes three ways in which laity have a part in the church's mission in virtue of their baptism. The first is the general service and witness of life and profession in the world. The second is the laity's cooperation with the hierarchy in works of the apostolate, such as Yves Congar had spoken of in relation to Catholic Action but not limited to this. The third is the mission assumed when the hierarchy designate a lay person to some spiritual office, such as that of presiding regularly at liturgical services in the absence of a presbyter. In the case of the second type of mission there is no reference in the Constitution to a mandate from the hierarchy, such as Congar had mentioned. Since the Council, writers usually speak of a mandate only with regard to the third kind of office, though of course the need of working with and under the hierarchy in the second case is always kept in mind. But this is a modification of Congar's position, in as much as he postulated that a mandate from the hierarchy was necessary to the ecclesial nature of such office.

The Conciliar Decree on the Apostolate of Lay People followed the same pattern as the Constitution on the Church. Even while introducing an acknowledgment of the particular charisms which are the source of special callings, it related these to the temporal order in which laity serve.[15] It certainly talks in no. 10 of the catechetical instruction provided by the laity within the community, but on the other hand the main teaching function of the laity is related to their competence in the temporal sphere.[16] In no. 17, the decree acknowledges that in some circumstances lay persons assume some of the functions and responsibilities of the clergy,[17] but its main concern is with their contribution to the building up of God's kingdom through social action and charitable works, whether this is done on a parish, diocesan, national or international level.

Perhaps what the Council had not clarified in a way sufficient to allow it to speak differently was the relationship of the church to the world. This was a theme that was explicitly addressed only in the last document of the Council, namely, the Constitution on the Church in the World, *Gaudium et Spes*. In the terms of this Constitution, there is no dualism between the secular and the sacred, between sacred ministry and service of the world. The church, which was defined by *Lumen gentium* as God's People, is here presented as the instrument of God's presence in the world for the sake of building up the kingdom of God. The church as a people bears responsibility for this mission, whether in its corporate stance or in the solidarity of the individual call of each and all of its members. Within this perspective, it might be possible to speak of the reciprocal responsibility of presbyter and lay person in the service of the one mission, rather than to pursue the implications of a distinction between presence in the ecclesial community and presence in the secular realm. The Council, however, did not leave itself time or opportunity to speak further to such questions.

As already noted, the Council had taken notice of the laity's active liturgical role even before writing the constitution on the church. First of all the conciliar documents was the Constitution on the Liturgy, wherein the principle of active lay participation was enunciated. This has had its effects particularly in the revision of the liturgical books and rites of the western churches.

In his work, *The Shape of Baptism*, Aidan Kavanagh has pointed to the far-reaching consequences which the implementation of the adult catechumenate can have for the entire style and reality of church community.[18] In effect, one of the things which the catechumenate needs is an expanding lay ministry. A fundamental principle of the new Rite of Christian Initiation of Adults is that the preparation of the candidates for initiation is the responsibility of the entire community. It is not one, however, to be carried out in a vague way, or as if there were nothing more than a prayerful concern with the welfare of the candidates at stake. A good catechumenal program needs some specific ministries. The rite itself mentions the role of godparents. To ask somebody to be sponsor for baptism has for too long been a social nicety, some way of complimenting a brother or a sister or a friend, or of obtaining social patronage for the child. In the revised rite for adults, it is a ministry of involvement in the spiritual journey of the catechumen. Since this requires charism and competence, it would be possible to envisage that the role of sponsor would develop as a stable ministry in a community, one for which a set group of persons would be chosen and prepared.

This is one good example of how new ministries emerge as the result of the implementation of liturgical renewal. As instructions on some of the other sacraments are put into effect, other examples will be apparent. Thus, marriage preparation requires an induction by the community, with special services designed to help the couple assume their covenant commitment as charism for the church and not merely as personal partnership. The care of the sick being the general context in which anointing takes place, services of comfort and healing are bound to take on added importance and even stability in ecclesial communities.

My earlier presentation of the German bishops' document showed how they relied on the distinction given in *Lumen gentium*. There has been a tendency on the part of the magisterium to employ this formula in regulating the renewal of ministries in the church. We find this, for example, in the words of Pope John Paul II in an address to priests in Mexico City, on the occasion of his visit there in 1979:

"You are priests and members of religious orders. You are not social directors, political leaders or functionaries of a temporal power. So I repeat to you: Let us not pretend to serve the Gospel if we try to dilute our charism through an exaggerated interest in the broad field of temporal problems. Do not forget that temporal leadership can easily become a source of division, while the priest should be a sign and factor of unity and brotherhood. The secular functions are the proper field of action of the laity, who ought to perfect temporal matters with a Christian spirit."[19]

Manifestly, the Pope is not here trying to restrict or define the role and activity of the laity, but he is addressing himself to the fact that in Latin America many priests are one with the revolutionary concern of the people in seeking a just order in society. It is on them that he wants to place some restrictions, and he does so by asking them to leave the temporal to the laity as their proper sphere of activity. Meeting for the conference at Puebla which was the occasion for the papal visit, the bishops of Latin America (CELAM) practically reiterated the Pope's words in speaking of priests. They also used the conciliar distinction, however, to tone down a tendency on the part of some laity to aspire to ministries within the church community rather than to employ their talent for the sake of the kingdom in the world.[20]

The participation of the laity in the mission of the church, especially in the construction of a world that befits human dignity and in the struggle against false values, is a topic to which Pope John Paul II often returns. Drawing out the conciliar teaching on the participation of the baptized in the prophetic, priestly, and kingly mission of Christ, he has taken note of the increasing number of ways in which the ministry of lay persons is taking shape. Thus, in addressing a gathering during a visit to Canada he quoted Romans 12.6–7 as text that casts light on the diversity and number of gifts by which the mission is enriched. Of these gifts that differ, he noted:

"Within the vast variety of the apostolate some are called to proclaim God's word as catechists, teachers or as those who lead adults through the rite of Christian initiation. Some will minister to families, the sick, the imprisoned, the disabled, youth or the aged. Some will assist in the area of social justice or health care or ecumenism. Others exercise administrative talents in diocesan or parish councils, or in the various organisms needed to involve the wider Christian community. Specialized movements of spiritual renewal for individuals and groups, especially for families, are able to contribute greatly to the church's mission."[21]

In the same discourse, the Pope took note of the laity's increasing involvement in a stable manner in full-time church ministry, carrying out pastoral tasks alongside bishops, priests, and deacons. Noting that this is "particularly providential" where there is a shortage of priests, he added that service of the gospel in one way or another is a permanent characteristic of the baptismal calling.[22]

Even with this insistence on the participation of the baptized in the ministry and mission of the church, however, John Paul II continues to interpret the lay vocation in the light of *Lumen Gentium* 31 and to insist on its essentially secular character. This accompanies an ever-growing stress on the special nature of the priestly calling and on the essential difference between ordained priesthood and the common priesthood of all the faithful. In confirming the choice of the laity's vocation and mission as the topic for the 1986 General Synod of Bishops, he returned to the distinction made in *Lumen Gentium* 31 as a guideline for the Synod's deliberations. On the one hand, he expressed the hope that through the workings of the Synod lay people would become more aware of "their essential inclusion in the church and of their responsible participation in its mission of salvation."[23] On the other hand, he intimated that it should help to clarify "the secular nature and task of the laity."[24]

To this clarification, however, he gave a positive rather than negative note, stating: "In the current state of the world, it is up to the laity to promote the indispensable alliance between science and wisdom, between technology and ethics, between history and faith, so that God's plan can be progressively carried out and with it humanity's true good can be achieved."[25]

The *lineamenta* drawn up by the Synod's general secretariate follow this inspiration.[26] This document quotes an array of texts from the documents of the Second Vatican Council on the calling and mission of the baptized, and is strongly affirmative of developments whereby new ministries have emerged in churches all around the world. In speaking, however, of the distinctive character of the lay vocation it refers primarily to *Lumen Gentium* 10 and 31, in an apparent attempt to lead to discussions that will avoid confusion between the ordained priesthood and lay ministries.[27] This, of course, is only a working document and has no authoritative bearing, but it is interesting to note that in addressing the distinction between the sacred ministry of those in order and the secular character of the laity's calling, it would exclude the possibility of taking this as a working distinction rather than as a theological one. It affirms that the conciliar distinction is not only a sociological datum, but a theological and ecclesial datum as well. Against this background, the particular "problem" to be faced by the Synod is stated as follows:

"The experience which in recent years some local churches have passed through urges renewed reflection on the ministries entrusted to the laity. Such reflection cannot avoid considering attentively the true nature both of the ecclesial 'ministry' in general, and, in particular, the ecclesial distinctiveness of the laity, especially their 'secular' condition. It is necessary to bear in mind that the term 'ministries' is sometimes used with a varying range of meanings.[28]

One can certainly see the point of such preoccupations. A certain kind of involvement by the presbyter in the social and political can take away from the place and role which he occupies in the Christian community. Likewise, if the laity were wholly caught up in the inner affairs of the church, this would take away in practice from the effective presence of Christian people in caring for temporal affairs, in the Spirit and according to the gospel of Christ. But one can wonder whether the distinction between sacred ministry and secular involvement even settles the practical concerns which it is intended to meet, let alone the theological problem. Indeed, it hardly seems to do so even on the part of those who have recourse to it, for in other matters they have to rely on other principles. Thus it becomes widely acknowledged and accepted, as we saw in the preceding chapter, that lay persons take on in some countries or even on whole continents many of the offices and functions attributed by theory to the clergy. Fostering lay ministries, then, means fostering lay leadership, and fostering lay leadership means fostering the lay presidency of whole communities of faith. Likewise, some political questions, such as a stand on human rights, are seen to be so important that they become the special duty not only of presbyters but indeed of bishops. Church leadership recognizes that it has to develop a position on social questions of all sorts, not only in theory but also in practice, and finds it hard to keep distinct the respective contribution of laity and bishop or presbyter in these matters. To allow the laity a part in party politics while denying it to bishops and presbyters, as the Puebla conference does,[29] sounds rather specious when the political polarizations are sharp—or, indeed, where political parties exist only in a suppressed state, as is the case for some of the countries addressed by CELAM.

60

Once again, it may be necessary to look at ecclesial polity and practice in order to develop a theology which meets the pastoral need of the moment. I pointed out that a major factor in the development of a theology such as that of Yves Congar, and eventually therefore that of the Vatican Council, was the fact of Catholic Action. Today, the main fact of the practical order which has similarly to be taken into account is probably that of the grass-roots Christian community, or *comunidad de base*. This teaches us that we cannot theologize about ministries except in the context of a Christian community which corporately assumes responsibility for its own community affairs and for the community's mission in the temporal and social arena. It teaches us that the structure of ministry is determined within such a community, on the basis of community need and personal charism, and not merely through the commissioning of single members, by whatever means chosen, whether it be ordination or mandate or blessing. It teaches us that we cannot develop parallel theologies of lay ministry and ordained ministry, but that we have to find a single theology of ministry, within which a theology of the sacrament of order itself may take on a new appearance. In other words, the practice of these grass-roots communities shows us that once the way is opened to lay ministry and responsibility, as indeed it had to be opened, nothing in ecclesiology is left untouched, and that the hierarchy too has to be ready to redefine itself. That, I believe, is the real meaning of the various attempts which I discussed in the last chapter to acknowledge charisms, distribute ministries, and define roles. The continuing resort to the distinction between the secular quality of the laity and the sacred ministry of the clergy, while it is sometimes no doubt the ploy of clerical power, is probably more fundamentally a concern that when it comes to define roles within the common mission of the church, we may do so in terms of the world which is to be redeemed and not only in the closet terms of a self-contained fraternity of pious interest.

61

Already in 1979, summing up three decades of theological writing on the laity, Rosemary Goldie noted the need to address this issue within a broader ecclesiology.[30] In particular, she indicated how important it was not to let the distinction between hierarchy and laity parallel that between the religious and the secular. All the ordained and all the laity are at one and the same time of the church and of the world, since it is the call of the church as a community to be the sacrament and instrument of the promotion of God's reign. With respect to the great variety of ministries exercised among lay people, Goldie asked that they all should be seen as ways of meeting God's call and serving the church's mission, without resorting to dogmatic or theological distinctions to differentiate them. Here she was referring to the tendency to give one theological qualification to a service, part-time or full-time, in pastoral ministry and another to the apostolate of a Christian presence in secular affairs. The only way to avoid such differentiation is to think in terms of the community and its life and mission, rather than in terms of isolated individuals, called or delegated to specific functions.

While the explosion of ministries continues apace on all continents, it is accompanied by a continuing explosion of theologies of ministry. Some of this literature is marked by a concern over the use of the term *ministry*, in an apparent attempt to limit its use to certain kinds of participation in the church's life.[31] Apparently, not all are willing to take Paul's generous if vague use of *diakonia* as a guideline. It may well be a difference in ecclesial polity that allows the issue to be seen differently in different parts of the world. The matter of right terms is more of a concern in the United States and in Germany than it would appear to be elsewhere. This can be linked to the difference between an organizational approach to ministry and one that is rooted in the life of basic Christian communities. While more and more people in the United States, for example, feel called to ministry, they tend to want a defined place within church structures to determine this calling. The issues of appointment, recognition, delegation, and nomenclature then become important. This would appear to be less an issue in churches where charisms and services are discerned and lived out within the life-boundaries of basic Christian communities, as on the Latin American continent. In that context, the more urgent question becomes one of realizing a community's nature as a eucharistic community, and so of the ordination of the leadership that would make this possible.

CONCLUSION

These first two chapters have selectively surveyed an agglomeration of theological opinions, documents and reports, but the basis of lay ministry, whether officially approved, granted by delegation, or merely exercised without formal designation by the church authorities, remains unclear. As an attempt at partial clarification, I can give a list of the degrees of recognition granted to these ministries, together with their apparent relation to baptism.

At the top of the ladder, there are the ministries of acolyte and lector, which are primarily liturgical offices but entail other charges as well. These are spelt out both as clearly enunciated offices in the church, and as distinctly lay. They belong to laity as such, yet require a special designation and installation or blessing to be assumed and exercised. In that sense, though predicated of the lay state as such, they are not offices common to all lay persons.

On the next rung, there are the extraordinary (special) ministers of communion. Here, the official documents seem to have substitution for the ordained clergy in mind, since there is emphasis on the extraordinary nature of the ministry. No doubt the Congregation for the Sacraments thought at first in terms of a substitution for, or assistance to, deacons and presbyters, but the coincidence of *Immensae caritatis* with *Ministeria quaedam* means in effect that this is a case also of lay persons substituting for other lay persons, namely, acolytes. Since handling the blessed bread and cup, and ministering them to others, could on a historical basis be seen as a ministry inherent to the lay state, it is not very clear why a special commission is needed or what it is intended exactly to signify. In other words, is it a matter of theological reasoning, or is it a matter of ecclesiastical discipline?

Thirdly, we could rank the many liturgical ministries of presidency which are exercised by women and men in various parts of the world, and which are accepted as part of a pastoral program by episcopacies, whether or not a special blessing is given when persons are appointed to these charges. On the one hand, this kind of presidency can be seen to be rooted in the charisms which flow from the grace of the Spirit given in baptism or chrismation. On the other hand, however, presidency is the very ground for the existence of a sacrament of order in the church. The main issue which arises from lay presidency is that of the relation between the ordained minister and the community, which is both a theological and a canonical question.

On the fourth rung of our imaginary ladder, I would place those offices occupied by lay persons in a more or less permanent fashion, and accepted as offices normal to the role of lay person. Such offices are well exemplified in the statement of the German episcopacy, already quoted. Some of these are said to belong more directly to the laity's mission of representing Christ in temporal concerns, others to constitute a help to presbyters and bishops, while still remaining distinctly lay offices. The rationale for these offices is clear enough and fits well with the general understanding of membership of the church. What is more problematic is which offices fit into the category of substituting for, or being delegated to, a function which is of itself proper to the sacrament of order. The most vexatious of these nondescript offices in some parts of the world is lay preaching, especially in the liturgical assembly. Is this something which it is normal for a lay person to do, always granted that it has to be in obedience to the hierarchy, or is it a clerical office, to which lay persons may be delegated, even at times suitably so?

If one climbs down to the fifth descending rung of the ladder, one will find the many occasional services, not involving office, rendered to one another by brothers and sisters in Christ, and without which no community could exist as such. How far these services extend, without encroaching on that territory which is proper to the sacrament of order, or without constituting a special, albeit lay, office, is not a query to which it is possible to give a clear and unambiguous answer. On the one hand, there is multiple encouragement to lay persons to develop the sense and the reality of service, but on the other there is the concern for ecclesial unity and ordering. Yet, one probably has to be very canonically minded to become anxious about such boundaries between service and order.

On the bottom rung, the one that is most down to earth, there is the daily Christian involvement in temporal affairs, called by the rather generic term of "witness," but obviously involving much sweat and tears if a person is to take unfailing cognizance of the gospel in all things. It is this which is rather constantly and consistently pointed to in magisterial documents on service and ministry as that which constitutes the basic function of lay Christians and the most important part of their Christian service, rendered in the name and in the love of Christ. In one mouth, this can sound like an admonition to the laity to keep to their place. In another, it is a cry of anguish, lest Christ be absent from the affairs of the world.

In the broad picture which I have sought to present, the questions raised by Paul VI's revision of the discipline of minor orders can be seen. The question is raised of the precise nature of lay sharing in the church's mission and ministry, as both complementary to and distinct from that of the ordained. The question is raised of the differentiation which is effected between ministries exercised by lay persons. The question is raised of the forms of recognition which are appropriately given to ministries, once they are differentiated. The question is raised of the relation between ministry in the liturgical assembly and other ministries, whether exercised by the same person or by different persons. The question is raised of the corporate responsibility of the entire ecclesial community's mission to the world and of the manner of its exercise. And finally, the question is raised of how and on what principles all ministry is structured and specific ministries undertaken.

These questions will be taken up again and answered insofar as possible in Chapter Five.

NOTES

1. E. Mersch, *The Theology of the Mystical Body*, translated by C. Vollert (Herder, St. Louis 1951).

2. Pius XII, "Litterae Encyclicae de Sacra Liturgia 'Mediator Dei,'" *Acta Apostolicae Sedis* 39 (1947) 521-600.

3. Thomas Aquinas, *Summa Theologiae* 3, 63.

4. *Summa Theologiae* 3, 72, 5.

5. Pius XII, op. cit. 555-557.

6. Yves de Montcheuil, *Aspects of the Church*, translated by A. LaMotte (Fides, Chicago 1955).

7. Pius XII, "Six Ans se Sont Ecoulés," *Acta Apostolicae Sedis* 49 (1957) 922-939.

8. Yves Congar, *Jalons pour une Théologie du Laicat*, Paris 1953. English translation: *Lay People in the Church*, revised edition (Newman Press, Westminster, Maryland 1967).

9. Op. cit., 173-187. Congar refers to the Augustinian synthesis in *De Civitate Dei* X, 6 (CSEL 40, 455).

10. Ibid., 308-313.

11. Karl Rahner, "Notes on the Lay Apostolate," in *Theological Investigations* II (Helicon Press, Baltimore 1963), 319-352.

12. Loc. cit.

13. Y. Congar, "The Church as People of God," *Concilium* 1 (Paulist Press, New York 1965), 16ff. For a study of the question before and during the Council, see M. Keller, "Theologie des Laientums" in J. Feiner-M. Löhrer, *Mysterium Salutis* 4/2 (Benziger Verlag, Einsiedeln 1973) 393-421.

14. Flannery 388-389.

15. Flannery 769.

16. Flannery 777.

17. Flannery 784.

18. Aidan Kavanagh, *The Shape of Baptism: The Rite of Christian Initiation* (Pueblo Publishing Company, New York 1978).

19. John Paul II, "Address to Priests in Mexico City," *Origins* 8 (1979) 548-549.

20. *Third Latin American Conference of Latin American Bishops, Evangelization at Present and in the Future of Latin America*, Official English Edition, (National Conference of Catholic Bishops, Washington D.C. 1979). Paragraph 815 of the document cites as a danger to be avoided "The tendency to clericalize the laity or to reduce the lay commitment of those who receive (pastoral) ministries. For that would overlook the fundamental mission of lay people, which is their involvement in temporal realities and their family responsibilities."

21. John Paul II in Canada, "The Laity's Call to Serve," *Origins* 14 (1984) 255f.

22. l.c. 256.

23. John Paul II to Synod Secretariate, May 19, 1984, *Origins* 14 (1984) 148f.

24. l.c.

25. l.c. 149. See also his address to the general assembly of the Pontifical Council for the Laity, November 19, 1984, *Documentation Catholique* LXXXII (1985) 35–37.

26. General Secretariate for the Synod of Bishops, *lineamenta* for the 1986 Synod, "The Laity's Vocation and Mission," *Origins* 14 (1985) 624–634.

27. l.c. 629.

28. l.c. 630.

29. See paragraph 524: "Party politics is properly the realm of lay people. Their lay status entitles them to establish and organize political parties, using an ideology and strategy that is suited to achieving their legitimate aims." Compare paragraph 526: "Pastors, on the other hand, must be concerned with unity. So they will divest themselves of every partisan political ideology that might condition their criteria and attitudes. They then will be able to evangelize the political sphere as Christ did, relying on the Gospel without any infusion of partisanship or ideologization."

30. Rosemary Goldie, "Lay, Laity, Laicity: A Bibliographical Survey of Three Decades," *The Laity Today: Bulletin of the Pontifical Council of the Laity* 26 (1979) 107–143.

31. For a suggested definition and a containment of the use of the term, cf. Thomas F. O'Meara, *Theology of Ministry* (Paulist, New York 1983) 134–175.

The Tradition

Chapter Three

On the Edges of History

What Paul VI did in his *motu proprio, Ministeria quaedam* of 1972, was to dismantle a clerical system which had begun in the Latin Church at the time of the papal decretals of the fourth and fifth centuries and was given its finishing strokes in the medieval period of Roman and Gallican canonical and liturgical intermingling. This development had its counterpart in other churches, both east and west of Rome. To grasp the full extent of the questions raised today by a revision of nonclerical ministries, it is necessary both to outline and to seek to interpret the history of this movement. If we can see what happened, and why it happened, we may be enriched by insight, through history, into what we are at present doing.

Two cautions need to be given from the start. The first is that it is rather a complex history, not one that is easy to summarize while maintaining both clarity and fidelity. The names and realities of ministry and office do not everywhere coincide. Even a simple term like *clergy* is not univocal. The second caution is that this history is not presented as a blueprint for modern times. There is no doubt a lesson to be learned from history, but it is not that of telling us what practices and offices are to be restored, in fidelity to earlier practices. It is a more subtle lesson, imposing on today's investigator the duty to seek to understand both what took place and why it took place, so that this understanding might provide some criteria for today's prudent and practical judgments.

A study of all the literature pertinent to the history of ministries in the early church, and scholarly criticism thereof, has been provided by A. Faivre.[1] But it seems to me that I can do enough for the interest of the possible readers of this book, if I examine the most basic document of all, namely, the *Apostolic Tradition* of Hippolytus, together with documents from the Syrian Church and from the western churches which can be linked in some way with Rome.

THE APOSTOLIC TRADITION OF HIPPOLYTUS OF ROME[2]
One of the most fascinating things about this document is that while it originated in Rome, its influence in later times is found chiefly in Syria and Egypt. Dispute about its authorship and dating will probably never end, but it is safe to take it as a document of the early third century and one which had considerable influence on church life. Apart from the *Didache*, it is the oldest extant document which sets out to give clear instructions on church order, with the avowed purpose of adhering to the apostolic tradition, even while in fact giving the force of "canonicity" to new church structures. What it portrays in effect is a church developing an ordered way of life, where functions, liturgies, services and ranks can proceed according to more or less stable regulations.

There is in the *Apostolic Tradition* a definite distinction between the clergy (*kleros*) and all other members of the community. This is the common name for bishops, presbyters, and deacons. Their distinctive role is said to be the performing of liturgy, and they are the only ones installed in office by a laying-on of hands (*cheirotonia*). In order to find the reason for the distinction between clergy and other members of the community, we must look at that passage of the treatise dealing with the installation of widows. This passage explains the distinction of office, the distinction in ways of installing persons in office, and the reasons for these distinctions:

72

"Let the widow be instituted by word only and let her be reckoned among the widows. But she shall not be ordained, because she does not offer the oblation nor has she a liturgical ministry. But ordination is for the clergy on account of their liturgical ministry. But the widow is appointed for prayer, and this is (a function) of all."[3]

Here it can be remarked that it is liturgical service which sets the clergy aside from all others. It is also noticeable that there are two distinct ways of appointing to office, the one by laying-on of hands, the other by installation (*katastasis*). What an installation "by word only" would be, today we are left to guess. Later documents do give prayers to be said over widows at their installation, but whether such prayers or some official naming are here meant we cannot say.

As well as the widow, another member of the church is said to be installed. This is the reader, who is appointed but does not receive the laying-on of hands.[4] A subdeacon is simply said to be named and he is ranked after the reader. Perhaps this shows even a third type of appointment, but it is not possible to be sure that installation and naming mean two different things.[5]

Three other persons are given special status in the document, but in each case it is pointed out that there is no official appointment involved since the foundation for this status is either charism, personal honor, or free choice. These three are the confessor, the virgin, and the one who has received the gift of healing. The first has gained personal honor by open and persevering profession of the faith. Hence, the confessor has a dignity equal to that of the presbyters and apparently takes his place among them.[6] The virgin acquires her place in the church order through personal choice, while healing is a charism given by the Spirit.

At this point, it is interesting to note the rather varied ways in which persons acquire their position in church order. The clergy, widows, readers, and subdeacons have their particular status because they are designated and are inducted by an appropriate rite. The confessor by reason of his fidelity in the faith is recognized as possessing a grace or a gift, comporting honor, which needs no further church recognition or appointment. The virgin's status is a result of personal choice, somewhat grudgingly noted in this official listing. The healer was probably one of several charismatics mentioned at this point in the treatise, part of which has been forever lost. Mention of him shows that recognition of the gifts of the Spirit is still accepted as a foundation for service in the community. In brief, then, official appointment, personal choice and the grace of the Spirit, manifested either in personal witness or in charismatic gifts, are the grounds on which persons serve the church and acquire rank in the community. This is an important point to note for an understanding of the subsequent history of ministry and office. Before speculating any further, however, it is better to say a word about the responsibilities of each of the groups mentioned.

The clergy are singled out on account of their official participation in liturgy, but the rest of the document shows that they have other and vaster responsibilities, as pastors, elders, teachers, and administrators. Indeed, presbyters exercise very little personal liturgical ministry. What stands out in the ordination of a presbyter is that the presbyterium was a collegial body offering advice and counsel to the bishop and people. There is something of a liturgization of office going on, so that all rankings find place in the assembly of worship. The office of presbyter, in other words, is not formally related to liturgical duties, but if he is to enjoy the respect of the people and if the meaning of his office is to appear in its full import, then he has to be given a liturgical assignment. Hence, in the assembly the presbyters act in unison with the bishop in extending hands over the gifts.[7] This is in itself an explanation of why the bishop is given his rank; it is on account of his liturgical ministry, even though he has considerable duties as pastor, teacher and administrator.[8] It is as if all other tasks have to be related to the liturgical, in order that their significance may appear and the honor and rank of the person holding office be established. This is of great interest, for it seems to show how distinctions came to be made in the church.

The reader also has a role in the liturgy, of which the book of readings given to him at his installation is the sign. He remains the most important of the lesser ministers who appear on the scene in the east, and here in the *Apostolic Tradition* he is ranked before the subdeacon. An obvious enough reason for his importance has to do with his ability to read the scriptures and to proclaim them in the assembly, for this would not have been a common accomplishment at the time. A further and greater reason has to do with the fact that the reading of the scriptures originally went with teaching and explaining them. Some modern writers draw a parallel between the reader and the charism of doctor (teacher).[9] What we have, then, in the *Apostolic Tradition* is not so much a recognition of this nonclerical ministry as a reduction of it to merely reading the scriptures and a control over even that, since it now requires official appointment. In the writings of Justin Martyr (c. 100-167), the teaching function is already reserved to the one who presides at the liturgy.[10] Later, the reader's function will itself be diminished, for the deacon will be confided with the proclamation of the gospel. The clergy—here that is the bishop, presbyter, and deacon—are extending their control and their authority at the expense of other gifted persons, and someone gifted in a way which could encroach upon this authority is not to be heard unless officially appointed.

The naming of a subdeacon to serve the deacon also seems to go along with a desire to put more order and distinction into church life, controlling even the lesser kinds of service in the liturgy and in other matters. The duties of helping with the gifts, keeping order in the assembly, or watching the doors are assigned to the subdeacon, lest they be left to chance. It is all too natural that a subdeacon become a likely candidate for clerical orders (according to the terminology of the *Apostolic Tradition*), and that his stint as subdeacon become a kind of apprenticeship.

The position given a widow shows another side to ranking in the church, not to be ignored in examining later developments. She is appointed not to any official liturgical function, but to personal prayer. This may seem odd at first on two counts. In the first place, widows had always been considered deserving of the church's charity and some of the gifts of the community went to them. Now, however, a distinction is made between widow in fact and widow in rank, for not all widows are allowed to belong to this rank. They have to prove themselves by long widowhood, and age has to be considered before one is appointed. The rather precise rules in the *Apostolic Tradition* are further elaborated in later and dependent literature. The second count on which the nomination may seem odd comes in the assertion that she is appointed to prayer, which is a duty common to all. If it is common to all, why should she be appointed to it? The reason seems to be that there is an incipient tendency to introduce a second kind of ranking into the community, alongside that of liturgical functions and ordination. This is a ranking based on spiritual perfection, if we are to judge from the two motives which seem to be behind the setting up of an order of widows.

From New Testament times all widows were accounted dependent on the church's bounty. Apparently there was also some desire to test the worthiness of the applicant for this charity. Virtue was expected of a widow, but some widows failed to live up to the rather demanding expectations of the community and of its leaders. A selection from among the widows to be cared for on the common budget would then be natural enough. This might not mean that others were completely neglected, but their claims on the community would have been less firm. A second motive for this distinction among widows had probably to do with the esteem for a life of asceticism and the efficacy attributed to the prayers of the devout. Hence their special place in the church.

At this stage, I want to return to the different grounds for ranking, namely, appointment, charism and personal choice. I do so to point out the priority given to the first over the other two, even though both of these had to have their part in the selection of bishop, presbyter and deacon. It is especially the relation between ordination and charism which is of interest. The confessor and healer probably represent an earlier stage of church life, when personal witness and charismatic gift could be grounds enough for holding office and authority, or when the church's intervention consisted mainly of a recognition of gifts of the Spirit and a channeling of their exercise. Now, while this recognition of gifts still plays its part, there is established the constant necessity of ordination for higher office. Ordination, not charismatic gift, becomes the definitive distinguishing mark in the church and the stamp of authority, even though the gifts of the Spirit are still considered necessary to the exercise of the office, as the ordination prayers show. Not only is order more highly structured, but as the case of the reader shows, the tendency is to submit even other services to tighter control. At the same time, charismatic gifts continue to be exercised, as the missing section of this document and the evidence of dependent documents, which will be examined later, would seem to indicate.

To sum up, then, the *Apostolic Tradition* cannot give us a complete picture of early church practice. It can only show that ministry, and even the life of prayer, were gradually being subjected to ordering and ranking.

THE SYRIAN CHURCH

Turning to the Syrian documents, which belong to the third and fourth centuries, we find these listings or rankings. The *Didascalia* lists bishop, presbyter, deacon, reader and widow, and augurs the institution of deaconess.[11] The *Apostolic Constitutions* list bishop, presbyter, deacon, deaconess, reader, subdeacon, cantor or psalmist, porter or doorkeeper, widow and virgin.[12] The *Testamentum Domini* lists bishop, presbyter, deaconess, reader and subdeacon.[13]

A first observation can be made about the use of the word clergy (*kleros*). The irony of its use in the *Apostolic Tradition* was that a term originally used to mark off believers from all others was there used to separate those selected for higher office from the other members of this same community of believers.[14] In these Syrian documents, the differentiation between clergy and laity is maintained, but the ranks of the clergy are extended beyond those of bishop, presbyter and deacon. The *Constitutions* explicitly include the deaconess and by prescribing a laying-on of hands for their installation implicitly include the reader and the subdeacon.[15] The *Testamentum Domini* goes along with the *Constitutions* in including the reader and subdeacon as clergy, but not in installing them through a laying-on of hands.[16] It may here be noted that the extension of the name *kleros* to include all those who perform any sort of liturgical service, however minor, goes still further in Syria about 380, according to the *Canones Apostolorum*, where the persons just mentioned, and the psalmist, are considered clerics.[17] It did not take long before the doorkeeper was added to their ranks.

There are two characteristics which together distinguish the clergy from other members of the church. The first is liturgical service, of whatever sort, the second that the bearer of the office receives sustenance from the community chest. Others, like widows, receive sustenance and support but since they have no liturgical function they are not clerics. The extension of the name cleric to include all manner of liturgical ministers indicates how much liturgy has been brought under the umbrella of the hierarchy. There are no longer roles for the ordained and for the laity in the liturgical ministry, but all liturgical ministry is clerical.

The contest between reader and subdeacon for priority of rank shows up in these writings. We know how it was resolved, when the subdeacon practically became a candidate for the higher orders. That this could happen to the reader as well is apparent in the admonition which the *Testamentum Domini* has the bishop address to him on his installation: he is to behave as one who makes himself worthy of higher office.[18] This sounds like the words of an arduous vocation director when faced with a good prospect.

Something more has to be said about the roles accredited to women. In the documents under discussion, the order of widows is given much the same place in the church, and for much the same reasons, as in Hippolytus. But the *Testamentum Domini* adds that a widow is expected on occasion to exhort disobedient women, to instruct the ignorant, to convert sinners, to attend the sick, to teach catechumens and assist them at baptism when they go into the pool, and to maintain discipline among her sex in the assembly.[19] None of these suggestions, however, should be allowed to obscure the fact that her contribution to the life of the church is given mainly in her prayer, which has its value on account of her ascetical and pious life. A woman would indeed have to be a veritable saint in order to win nomination, if she is to be a widow who lives up to what the author expects her to be: pious, persevering in carrying her cross, a good mother to her orphaned children, much seen at prayer, comforter of the afflicted, gentle and sweet-tempered, poor in fact and in spirit, a hard-worker, joyful without ostentation—and more besides. All of this of one person!

It is, however, through the order of deaconess that women have access to the ranks of the clergy and that their office in the liturgy is established. The deaconess, according to the *Didascalia* and the *Constitutions*, is confided with many of the duties assigned to widows by the *Testamentum Domini*. But she is a member of the clergy, and receives the laying-on of hands because of her liturgical functions, it would seem. These functions are the duty to assist women at baptism when they go down into the pool, and to keep order in the assembly, particularly among the women.

Since these are not the only documents from the early centuries which mention the deaconess, there is naturally some discussion among scholars about her place in the hierarchy or, more generally, in the ministry.[20] It would be anachronistic to ask whether she received the sacrament of order, but one can ask more pertinently whether she is to be listed among the top offices or among the lesser, and whether she equals in rank her male counterpart, the deacon. In the final analysis, it would seem that she belonged to the lesser clergy and was not admitted to all the liturgical functions of the deacon, especially those connected with the eucharist. This is not to offer any argument pertinent to the role of women in today's church, since that question is not to be decided on the sole basis of what was done in days of yore. It is simply to be as accurate as possible in recounting the facts of history.

Mention of the virgins among the orders of the church is further evidence of the hierarchy of spiritual perfection, when it is attached to a way of life, such as that of virginity or of widowhood.

Charismatics also have their place in these lists. The *Testamentum* speaks of healing, knowledge, and tongues as charisms to be honored, though they do not rank those who possess them among the orders of the clergy and they are not offices in which one can be installed.[21] The *Apostolic Constitutions* explicitly state that the exorcist is not a member of the clergy nor an office. It is rather a gift that has to be put to the test by its fruits.[22]

Are these charismatic services mentioned in the documents because they were of special importance? Or are they mentioned for another reason, namely, that some who claimed these gifts were moved by a desire for the dignity and the financial support due an office in the church? In this latter case, it may be the intention of the canonical author to exclude those of unworthy motives from such privilege, even while seeming to honor the charismatic gifts themselves. At any rate, one can say that from the evidence of the Syrian documents it can be seen that charisms were still exercised freely in the church but were being gradually subjected to greater control and supervision, without ever being allowed to rank alongside those offices which were granted only by appointment.

THE ROMAN CHURCH[23]
In a letter of Bishop Cornelius of Rome to Bishop Fabius of Antioch in 251 A.D., cited by Eusebius in his *Ecclesiastical History*,[24] it appears that the Roman Church at that time had forty-six presbyters, seven deacons, seven subdeacons, forty-two acolytes, fifty-two exorcists, readers and doorkeepers, and one thousand five hundred widows and indigent. This same list, with the addition of virgins and confessors of the faith, appears in the Good Friday orations of the *Gelasian Sacramentary* in the eighth century.[25] It cannot be concluded, of

course, that such lists of offices and orders in the church remained the same for all these centuries. Readers and exorcists, in fact, disappear from some listings between 251 and 900, most probably because their duties were absorbed into the higher orders. That they did reappear and finally became a permanent heritage of the Roman Church in later centuries, was probably due to Gallican influence.

The letter of Cornelius predates the better known papal decretals of the fourth and fifth centuries.[26] What it says of church order in Rome is quite different from what we found in Hippolytus, who also professes to speak for Rome. Can one imagine such changes taking place in the short half-century between the two documents? However one explains it, a comparison with Cyprian's Carthage suggests that quite rapid changes did take place in church order at that time, due to the increasing exchange between the civil power and the ecclesiastical power. Though persecutions had not come to a close, from a community of worship and fraternal charity the church was becoming a more visible and authoritative body, needing the kind of structure which would uphold its new position.

As noted, the differences between the *Tradition* and later documents are considerable. In Cornelius's day, less emphasis seems to be placed on liturgy as the dividing factor between clergy and laity, and this is certainly true of later Rome. Full commitment to the church's administration is as much a reason why someone belongs to the clergy as is liturgical ministry or service of the altar. The hierarchy of bishop, presbyter and deacon of course remains paramount, but even there one finds, as in the *Verona Sacramentary*,[27] that much stress is placed on the bishop's *auctoritas* and *potestas* or on the presbyter's dignity and honor, rather than on their position as servants in the community.

In the church of Rome the name of clerk, or cleric, from being a generic name for everyone holding ecclesial office, became a word to designate a state in itself, which could be acquired by anyone who was accepted into the papal service, provided he in turn accepted the duties of the office and its way of life. From being tonsured, which became the normal process for becoming a cleric, one could hope to ascend along the scale of honors to the higher rungs. A whole range of rules and expectations came into force over a couple of centuries and under the Constantian peace these were enforced by the civil privileges given to clergy so that the *cursus honorum* of the clergy assumed a physiognomy very similar to that of the civil service. Ascent in the ranks was designed to develop worthy ministers, but the process was very like that used by the state, even down to the vocabulary.

The very name *clericus* or *clericatus* eventually became more and more a term to distinguish the lesser orders or offices (*officia*) from the higher orders or ministries (*ministeria*). A strange history indeed for a word that in early Christian Greek meant all God's chosen people, that is, "selected ones." The term came to be applied to higher liturgical ministers, then to all who have liturgical office and church support, and finally in its Latin form to those who live by the service and support of the church, other than the higher liturgical ministers.

Finally, it became practice, and even law, that anyone in the service of the papal household and the administration of the church should be a cleric rather than a layman. This was the step taken under Pope Gregory the Great, who professed himself shocked to see young laymen working as valets in the papal chamber.[28] Judging from the Roman *Ordines*, the odd layman remained around the papal household, as a servant in less intimate relation to the papal person, or perhaps working in the notary office or the treasury, but since most of these functions were taken over by clerics he became a rather rare breed. Majordomo, officials in the treasury, notaries and defenders of the papal person, did not have to be clerics by nature of these offices, yet they seem to have been more often clerics than laymen from the time of Gregory onward, which is to say from quite early in the history of such offices. They came into existence only because of the expanding burden of administration in an expanding papacy.

Widow and virgin are names that appear in the lists of orders, where they stand as reminders of the continuing importance given to lives of chastity, asceticism and prayer, especially when exemplified in a way of life publicly professed. Indeed, this esteem for spiritual perfection and its public character is mixed up with the decretal laws which brought the *cursus* of the clerical state into being. The reasons why at first conjugal abstinence and later celibacy were imposed on those in major orders were their sacramental ministry and a congruent life of prayer.[29] It was the hope that only those would be ordained to these offices who fitted high expectations, which warranted that celibacy be eventually imposed further down the line, as for subdeacons, or that at least men be put to the test in lower ranks before acceding to the higher. While therefore it is rightly remarked that not all the clergy had liturgical functions, it remains true that the existence of clerics in such numbers, or the kind of life expected of them, was governed by the sacralization of liturgy and its ministers. The *sacerdotium*, inclusive of both sacramental power and ecclesial authority, extended out to embrace many lesser functions and lesser ranks, all in the interest of underscoring its own primacy and nobility.

The question now arises: do the offices which came to be clericalized and ranked as orders have roots in ministries that members of the community once performed without official appointment or ordination? There are not many easy answers to such a question, given the sparse documentation on church life and order of the early centuries of Christianity. Just a certain amount can be documented, and the rest conjectured.

The first information we have about the acolyte is that he was a messenger. This was the role in which acolytes served Cyprian at Carthage.[30] Bringing the *fermentum* to the presbyters in the *tituli* of Rome, according to the practice known to us from Innocent I, [31] is not far removed from such an original task. Perhaps the acolyte was rather a clerical figure from the start, in the sense that he was always a servant to bishops and deacons, not of course in the sense that the clerical state and distinction of later days are to be read back to the origins of the office of acolyte. But he was a ready candidate for inclusion in the ranks of clerics. He finally wound up as minister to the deacon at the altar.

The reader was an accomplished person, as already noted in discussing the *Apostolic Tradition*. He not only read the scriptures in the assembly, but could also be a teacher, instructing the faithful in the knowledge of them. Origen, a learned doctor with his own school, not merely read but at Caesarea actually expounded the scriptures in the church assembly while still a layman.[32]

Exorcism of evil spirits, as pointed out in the *Apostolic Constitutions*, was a gift that could not be given at the will of the church, for it was of the Spirit. This also seems to be how Tertullian saw it.[33] The power to combat evil spirits is not something that can be channelized as the church wills or her authority decrees. The catechumenate of the fourth and fifth centuries played a part in formalizing and ritualizing the practice of exorcism.[34] The irony of this is that when a formal office of exorcist came into existence, the incumbent faced the devil only under these rather antiseptic conditions.

Anything more dreadful had to be referred to the bishop.

Of the doorkeeper it can only be said that his office is a practical necessity. Since his duty is to be guardian of the sacred places, it is also one that was readily clericalized.

OTHER WESTERN CHURCHES

There is similarity between the offices of Rome and other western churches, but not uniformity. Thus the canons and ritual books of the Spanish and Gallican churches mention some offices never ranked in the history of Rome in the clerical lists. These are the office of psalmist or cantor, that of excavator of burial places (which is how I translate the Latin word *fossores*, since these *fossores* clearly did more than modern gravediggers) and that of keeper of the books. Since these were offices to which people could be named and inducted by the presbyter in a small community rather than by the bishop, they are evidence that the distribution of offices was not as tied to the cathedral as in Rome.[35]

Oddly enough, the fifth-century Gallican treatise, *Statuta Ecclesiae Antiqua*,[36] which had so much influence on Roman practice in the middle ages, probably does not represent the Gallican system of the fifth century when it was written or compiled. Like much else in the treatise, the system of ecclesiastical orders which it gives is less the reality than a traditionalist's reforming intention. This is true even though the writer gives not only a description of each order but also the rite of ordination. How much he relied on the way the rites were actually carried out and how much he himself composed is not a question that can be fully resolved. In any case, in this treatise we do find the clerical list of bishop, presbyter, deacon, subdeacon, acolyte, exorcist, reader and doorkeeper, together with the rites of ordination. As a parish office, to be disposed of by the presbyter in charge, the treatise mentions the cantor or psalmist. The orders, it will be immediately recognized, are the seven which were definitively canonized in medieval Rome and worked into the Roman Pontifical, there remaining until a few years ago.

DIAGNOSING THE PROCESSES OF CHANGE

Such, then, is the history of a development which gradually institutionalized all liturgical ministries and even in the spiritual life set up a hierarchy of orders in the churches. Any kind of official service of the church was put under the command of the *sacerdotium*. Liturgical offices were somehow subsumed under the exercise of the priesthood of the altar. Administrative offices, of however small a kind, were by their clericalization subjected to and given status under the authority of the episcopacy.

When St. Thomas Aquinas wrote his theology, the clerical *cursus* seemed so much part of tradition that he could write of the minor orders of porter, reader, exorcist, and acolyte that they were an apportioning of the original functions of the deacon to meet the demands of an expanding cult.[37] Each of them could be in some way related to the service of the eucharist, this being of the essence of an order in the church. Since by Thomas's time the psalmist and the cantor had ceased to be considered orders, he justified this by saying that theirs was a function which belonged to all the people, or at least to the choir.[38]

In practice, of course, by that time the minor orders did not mean very much. They were steps on the way to the priesthood, or ranks given to persons in the service of an episcopal curia. Some consideration was given to their revival in parish ministry at the time of the Council of Trent.[39] In its reform decrees, there was a proposal to make ordained clerics of the lesser persons active in the celebration of the liturgy, so as to give more dignity to worship. In other words, this proposed reform was part of the Council's intent to do away with the abuses of undignified celebration of the Mass. The two functions thought particularly useful were those of acolyte and reader. It was even suggested that when no cleric was available, suitable laymen could discharge these functions. The proposal, however, came to nothing and the minor orders remained on the books but received no notice except in the seminaries, which Trent did so much to foster.

In some respects, the subsumption of liturgical offices into the priesthood was even greater in the east than in the west. Though these churches are quite traditional and retain the orders listed in the early canonico-liturgical books, they came to look upon the offices of reader and subdeacon as part of the priesthood. These two offices are conferred with a laying-on of hands, and recorded rites for the conferral of the office of reader explicitly refer to its part in the priesthood. Thus, for example, in the collection of rites for the Byzantine church made in the seventeenth century by J. Goar, the office of reader is explicitly called the first step of the priesthood.[40]

To understand how much these traditions of east and west represent a formalization or clericalization of roles and ministries, which virtually excludes the laity from liturgical services, it is necessary to get some feel for the pre-Nicene church. There is not much documentation to which to appeal, but something can be gleaned from odd pieces of information as well as from what carries over from early practices into the period of formalization. For instance, a homily of St. John Chrysostom mentions certain early practices that were still in vogue in his time, which allows us to suspect that he was referring to a fuller sharing of the faithful in church ministries, both charismatic and general.

"There are occasions [says Chrysostom] when there is no difference at all between the priest and those under him: for instance, when we are to partake of the awful mysteries; for we are all alike counted worthy of the same things . . . before all one body is set and one cup. And in the prayers also, one may observe the people contributing much. For in behalf of the possessed, in behalf of those under penance, the prayers are made in common. . . . The offering of thanksgiving again is common: for neither doth he [the celebrant] give thanks alone, but also all the people. For having first taken their voices, next when they assent that it is 'meet and right so to do,' then he begins the thanksgiving. . . . Now I have said all this in order that each of the laity also may keep their attention awake, that we may understand that we are all one body, having such difference among ourselves, as members with members, and may not throw the whole upon the priests; but ourselves also so care for the whole Church, as for a body common to us."[41]

The point to underline through this quotation is that the liturgy was the affair of all the people, and this in a context within which the church itself was the affair of all the people. Whatever were the special gifts of each or the specific roles of some, the church in early centuries kept a prevailing sense of being one body, "having such difference among ourselves, as members with members."

It is then more comprehensible that we should find certain indications that the assignment of roles did not mean a monopoly or special privilege with respect to the sacraments or any other ministry. In these days when the nomination of special ministers of the eucharist is still a problem, it is good to remember that in early times the faithful took the holy bread home with them, so that they might take communion during the week.[42]

Eusebius in telling a story about an old man, Serapion, taken with mortal illness, gives an instance of a young boy taking communion to his dying grandfather.[43] Writing about 410 A.D., Innocent I lets us glimpse a tradition whereby people took the holy oils home and anointed one another for relief from various kinds of ailments, even though a more solemn form of anointing by bishop or presbyter was the recommended practice.[44] Even such a highly organized program and ceremonial as the catechumenate of the fourth and fifth centuries can be understood only as a ritualization and formalization of a process of ministering in which the whole body of the church was involved, by both common concern and special ministries.

The writings of St. Basil of Caesarea often refer to the tension between charismatic principle and the need for church order.[45] His teaching on the Holy Spirit is the main factor in his ecclesiology. The church is a communion in the love inspired by the Spirit, who is given to all in baptism, together with the knowledge of Christ and of mysteries. He is also the source of gifts or charisms, so that the community is enriched by many services. This is the principle. In practice, Basil seems to have been more at home with the use of charisms in the ascetical brotherhood which followed his Rule of Life than he was with their use in the body of the church as a whole. In the brotherhood, he could be sure of a mortified life, of obedience to elders and to leaders, and of a testing of spirits. Among the faithful abiding in the world, not all could be expected to withstand blandishments or resist false teachings. Consequently, the charism of leadership is most often stressed in Basil's works. This is the sign to look for in candidates for the episcopacy, as it is to the bishop that the church can look for leadership in word and in government. Obedience to him becomes the touchstone.

Basil moreover looked to the ascetical brotherhood to produce the bishop and all the ministries needed by the church. The demand for virtue, and indeed for celibacy, in ministers led to an easy clericalization of ministries. The convergence established by Basil between a hierarchy in the spiritual life and the hierarchy of ministry is remarkable. He looked upon lesser orders as the breeding ground of worthy candidates for the higher offices, and was quite severe on those who seemed to seek entry into their ranks more to enjoy clerical privilege that out of a desire to serve.

It may be that the fifth-century work of the Pseudo-Dionysius gives us the best picture of the mentality which is responsible for these developments which we have outlined, and Faivre has perceptively included an *excursus* on him in his detailed study of canonical and liturgical literature.[46] This pseudonymous author had a hierarchical vision of the whole of creation. God posited everything and every person in their proper place, and it is only by keeping this arrangement intact that it is possible to attain perfection. He introduced the word *hierarchy* into discussion of ministry in the church, and extended the vocabulary of *liturgy* to include the functions of the lower orders as well as those of bishop, presbyter and deacon.

He describes both the hierarchy of ministry and the hierarchy of perfection, which the hierarchy of ministry serves. In this latter, the single state of widowhood or virginity, and especially the monastic state, have pride of place. In the former, all orders descend from the episcopacy. He even looks for a parallel between this earthly hierarchy and the heavenly hierarchy of angels, thus showing that the order of the church is made in heaven. In the process, he relates the church's ministry much more to the altar than to the community, since the hierarchy of creation exists to the glory of God and its principal service is to honor God.

Pseudo-Dionysius makes an extreme application of a principle enunciated in such an early document as *First Clement*, namely, that in the assembly each one should keep the place assigned to him, for it is assigned by God.[47] Our fifth-century writer wants to see this applied even to the services of the burial of the dead, when the body of the deceased is to be placed in the part of the church which the person occupied when living. Apparently it is to be presumed that this marks his or her place also in heaven.

There is some verbal similarity between the first-century and the fifth-century authors in their appeal to a divine order, but the mentalities are completely different. Their attitudes show how great were the changes that had taken place in the interim. For the author of *First Clement*, the commanding symbol of holiness is the holy people. God's glory is in them and they are his fitting worship. As the letter's great prayer expresses it, there is a reflection and sharing of divine glory in the people who are saved, in the authority of their leaders, and even in the authority of earthly rulers.[48] The holiness of God is indeed awesome and tremendous, but it becomes close to us in the lives of his saints and in the works of creation. For the second of our two authors, Pseudo-Dionysius, the principal symbol of the holy is the altar and glory is rendered to God primarily through the exercise of the office of the priesthood. It is only by much purification that one can merit to enter into the sanctuary, there to give honor and praise to God. The order of ministries through which a candidate ascends is meant to gradually purify him, so that he may become worthy to enter into the enlightenment of the priestly liturgy and carry out the actions or service that God has ordained.

In light of what has been said, it is possible to ask what is the full import of the reforms made by Paul VI in *Ministeria quaedam*. The desire to see the ministries of acolyte and reader, along with other possible ministries, designated as lay offices and not clerical, is indeed to harken back beyond the age of clericalization. But one might also in the light of history understand the acrimony of the French bishop's request in 1970 to be enlightened on the difference between the institution of acolyte and the designation of special ministers of the eucharist. True indeed it is that in the earliest documents the lower orders were not clerical, certainly not seen as part of the priesthood,[49] but there is in the case of nonclerical roles a tendency to formalize and order services which had probably been more indebted to the graces of the Spirit and an informal recognition thereof in earlier times. This goes along with a tendency to limit to the few certain offices which had, at least to some extent, belonged to the many. This tendency is exemplified in the restriction of the practice of lay persons carrying the sacred host home to communicate themselves or others, the ministry of communion being limited to instituted or ordained ministers. Faced with what is said in *Ministeria quaedam* and the history to which it makes explicit appeal,[50] we are forced to ask how the recognition of the service of the laity can be advanced by the institution of special ministries, or by their liturgical installation, especially when they touch on matters which are common to all rather than peculiar to the few.

The first thing to be done in regard to ministry is to prevent the sacrament of order from swallowing up all ministries. This Paul VI and his reforms have attempted to do. The second thing is not to take the reasons for the sacrament of order and use them to justify a proliferation of distinctions among the laity. This perhaps remains a problem in the new canonical and liturgical discipline of ministries.

The sacrament of order can best be understood as a necessary evolution in the church. In recent years it has been pointed out that there has to be a correspondence between presidency in the community and presidency in the liturgy, and this is well and good, for so it ought to be. It is even correct to state that one goes from the former to the latter, and not vice versa. Yet, it is only in relationship to the eucharist that we can understand the reason for and meaning of ordination, and understand too that it became necessary in time, rather than being necessary from the beginning. This necessity belongs to the community demand for ritual, to the need to express the worshiping community's sense of the presence of its Lord, and of the sense of being but one community in the communion of an apostolic tradition and in the communion of the one body throughout the churches. It is due to charism and the Spirit that the one who presides in charity and in the eloquence of teaching should also preside in the celebration of the Lord's Supper. It is a matter of ritual and sacrament that his presiding action be recognized as the Lord's action at the Supper which continues in his church. The ritualization of the words of Christ as recorded in the narrative of the Supper and the need for a ritual of ordination seem to belong together. It is remarkable that in the eucharistic prayers of the churches the institution narrative which occurs in indirect discourse is the section of the prayer which becomes the object of ritualization, with the result that the very words are almost lifted out of context. This is not, at least in the first instance, because of any particular power attributed to these words, but because their repetition by the presider, and the repetition of the actions accompanying them, are the ritual guarantee of the Lord's presence and of the continuity of the worshiping assembly with the gathering of the disciples around the Lord on the night before he died. To this ritualization

94

there corresponds the need to ordain by a laying-on of hands to the office of eucharistic presidency. If the presbyter and the deacon are included, it is because of their proximity to that action. It is also a legitimation through the eucharist of the place granted them in the life of the church.

Now what seems to occur is that this process of inclusion or legitimation can keep on growing. It can be used to justify the bishop's tendency to assert a monopoly over many ministries, keeping them to himself. It can also be used to keep control over other ministries and ways of life, both within and without the liturgical assembly. The tendency to institute first, and then to ordain, ministries such as that of reader, or persons such as widows and deaconesses, is nothing other than a way of restricting ministries and privileges through giving them a special ritual significance, or even a quasi-sacramental significance. There is a clear reason and necessity for a sacrament which ordains to the presidency of the eucharist, stated indeed not in terms of power but of meaning, but is there a reason for liturgically instituting a reader?

In using the title *On the Edges of History* for this chapter, by history I mean what is written. In other words, history when it is written is an act of interpretation, neither a full nor a direct account of what took place in people's lives. So far, history of the church has been written mostly as the story of bishops and priests and popes. They are the holders of power, and the story of a society is told in terms of the exercise of power. The story of "other" ministries is usually limited to narrating their subordination to the priesthood.

Perhaps history is now taking a new turn. What has been on the edges may move toward the center. Such a history would be written with different views of the church community, different images of power. It might well turn out to be a history with an edge of sadness to it. The sadness would be caused by the realization that certain forces in the life of the church went unexplored or unused. The sadness would also be interpretation, and so belongs in history. It is not always possible to argue for present reform from what was done in the past, or if we read documents only to find out what they say and not what they mean. The clergy did indeed "overpower" the laity, ministries were monopolized. Women did not hold an important place in the power structure of the church. The process is documented. When we see why these things were so, or what happened to make them so, we begin to understand. From that basis, it is possible to talk to the present.

NOTES

1. A. Faivre, *Naissance d'une Hiérarchie: les Premières Etapes du Cursus Clérical* (Beauchesne, Paris 1977). The bibliography runs from p. 15 to p. 30, inclusive.

2. I use the English translation made by Gregory Dix and reissued by H. Chadwick, *The Treatise of the Apostolic Tradition of St. Hippolytus of Rome* (SPCK, London 1968), while keeping an eye on *La Tradition Apostolique de Saint Hippolyte: Essai de Reconstitution* by Bernard Botte (Aschendorf, Münster 1963).

3. Dix 20-21.

4. Ibid., 22.

5. Faivre, 52, argues that they do.

6. Dix 18-19.

7. On the presbyters, cf. Dix 13-14 and 6.

8. See the ordination prayer, ibid., 4-6.

9. See Faivre 58-62.

10. I Apol. 67.

11. R. H. Connolly, *Didascalia Apostolorum: the Syriac Version translated and accompanied by the Verona Latin fragments, with an Introduction and Notes* (Clarendon Press, Oxford 1929).

12. *Constitutions of the Holy Apostles,* translated and edited, with notes, by James Donaldson, in *The Ante-Nicene Fathers* (Charles Scribner's Sons, New York 1925) Vol. VII. Book VIII contains the section on orders, pp. 492–493. The Council of Laodicea, held between 344 and 360 A.D., lists in canon 24 the ecclesiastical ranks of presbyter, deacon, subdeacon, reader, singer, exorcist, doorkeeper, and the order of ascetics. Cf. *Canones Apostolorum et Conciliorum,* ed. H. Bruns (Turin: Bottega d'Erasmo 1959) 75–76. The Pseudo-Ignatius of the mid-fourth century lists presbyters, deacons, subdeacons, readers, psalm-singers, doorkeepers, gravediggers, exorcists, confessors, deaconesses, virgins, and widows as the orders of the church. Cf. Pseudo-Ignatius, *Ad Antiochenos* 12 (PG 5,908).

13. I. Rahmani, *Testamentum Domini Nostri Jesu Christi* (Hildesheim 1968). There is an English translation: J. Cooper and A. J. MacLean, *The Testament of the Lord* (T. & T. Clark, Edinburgh 1902).

14. See I. de la Potterie, "L'origine et le sens primitif du mot laic," *Nouvelle Revue Théologique* 80 (1958) 840-853.

15. *Constitutions* 492, 493.

16. *Testamentum* 44-45.

17. See Faivre, 140-141.

18. *Testamentum* 44. See *Didascalia* 130-145 on widows.

19. *Testamentum* 128-131: on the conduct expected of widows, see 94-97.

20. The principal monograph on the subject is R. Gryson, *The Ministry of Women in the Early Church,* translated from the French (Liturgical Press, Collegeville 1976).

21. *Testamentum* 108-109.

22. *Constitutions* 493.

23. For a brief survey, see B. Fischer, "Esquisse historique sur les Ordres Mineurs," *La Maison-Dieu* 61 (1960) 58-69.

24. *The Ecclesiastical History of Eusebius Pamphilus,* translated from the original with an introduction by Christian Frederick Cruse (Baker Book House, Grand Rapids 1977) 265.

25. L. C. Mohlberg, *Liber Sacramentorum Romanae Aeclesiae Ordinis Anni Circuli* (Herder, Rome 1960) n. 404.

26. Faivre studies these in detail, 309-336.

27. L. C. Mohlberg, *Sacramentarium Veronense* (Herder, Rome 1956) nn. 947, 954.

28. See M. Andrieu, *Les Ordines Romani du Haut Moyen Age* (Spicilegium Sacrum Lovaniense, Louvain 1960) Vol. 2, 40-41.

29. See R. Gryson, *Les Origines du Célibat Ecclésiastique du premier au septième siècle* (J. Duculot, Gembloux 1970).

30. See Faivre 307.

31. *Epistola ad Decentium*, XXV, V, 8: PL 20, 556-557.

32. Eusebius, loc. cit., 240.

33. See Faivre 187.

34. See A. Kavanagh, *The Shape of Baptism*, 167-168.

35. See *Liber Ordinum*, ed. M. Férotin (Paris 1904).

36. *Statuta Ecclesiae Antiqua*, ed. Ch. Munier (Presse Universitaire de France, Paris 1960).

37. *Summa Theologiae*, Supplementum 37, 2, ad. 2.

38. Ibid., ad 5.

39. *Concilii Tridentini Acta* (ed. Soc. Goerresiana 1924) vol. VI, 598, 627-628.

40. J. Goar, ed., *Euchologion seu Rituale Graecorum*, Paris 1647; Venice 1731; (phot. reprint Graz 1960) 197. Rites for the Maronites, East and West Syrians and the Copts may be found in E. Martène, *De antiquis Ecclesiae ritibus*, liber 1, c. 18, art. 11, Antwerp 1763, vol. 2, 95-120.

41. John Chrysostom, Hom. XVIII in 2 Cor., par. 3, *Library of the Fathers of the Holy Catholic Church* (Oxford 1848), vol. 27, 216-217.

42. *Apost. Trad.*, Dix 36, 37.

43. Eusebius, loc. cit., 267-268.

44. Innocent I, *Ep. ad Decentium*.

45. On Basil of Caesarea, see P. J. Fedwick, *The Church and the Charisma of Leadership in Basil of Caesarea* (Pontifical Institute of Medieval Studies, Toronto 1979): Faivre 223-228.

46. Faivre 172-180.

47. 1 Clement 40, 2-6: ed. K. Lake, *The Apostolic Fathers* (London 1959) Vol. 1, 76-79.

48. English text in L. Deiss, *Springtime of the Liturgy* (Liturgical Press, Collegeville 1979) 82-85.

49. A study of the concept of priesthood as used of the clergy belongs in a work on the sacrament of order. See David N. Power, *Ministers of Christ and His Church* (Geoffrey Chapman, London 1969) 38-39.

50. *Rites* 726.

Chapter Four

Learning from the New Testament

At one time in Roman Catholicism it was common to
think that church institutions, in order to be authentic,
had to be identified in the New Testament, at least in
embryo. In the opinion of many authors sorting out the
facts about the source, nature, exercise and transmission
of ministry in New Testament times meant finding what
was necessary to the church and how ministry and authority were to be transmitted. In this way, the hierarchical institution of bishop, presbyter and deacon were
traced back to divine institution, and charismatic ministries could be easily distinguished from the hierarchical.
Despite this rather common point of view, the church
remained cautious and circumspect in her dogmatic or
other official declarations. Both Trent and Vatican II
wanted to confirm and affirm the authority of bishops
and their ordained helpers, but they refrained from stating that this kind of ministry is found in its identical
form in apostolic times. Both Councils restricted themselves to asserting the legitimacy of the hierarchy and
the fact that it is they who, in the present times, hold the
authority and power of Christ.

WHAT MINISTRIES?
Without, therefore, questioning the legitimate authority
of the episcopacy, both ecumenical dialogue and exegetical studies now make it possible for Catholics to inquire
into the reality and possibility of other types of church
ministry. Studies of ministry in the New Testament
seem to indicate that it is next to impossible to give a
clear factual description of the state of ministries in that

era.[1] Much of the information about the facts comes from Paul's letters or from those which lay claim to his authority. Other sources are scattered through the Acts of the Apostles and the Catholic epistles. Certain episodes told in the gospels, such as the sending of the seventy-two in Luke 10.1-20, are apparently influenced by later church structures. A harmonious system cannot be found on the basis of this evidence, nor can a complete and exhaustive list of services be drawn up.

Some scholars have tried to make sense out of the New Testament evidence by contrasting the formation of ministries in the Palestinian church with the evolution that took place in the churches claiming Paul's authority. Others look to the differences between Jewish Christianity and Hellenistic Christianity, or contrast the Pauline and the Johannine churches. All of this helps to some extent, mostly because it pinpoints the diversity of earliest Christian times. In fact, exegetical studies have put their finger on the diversity and indeterminacy of ministries in the early church. This very diversity suggests that the Spirit's creativity, and the church's response to it, has had much to do with the formation of ministries and can continue to give rise to new forms of ministry.

A necessary principle of interpretation is that the community is prior to its ministers. Even the importance of the group of the Twelve in the New Testament shows this priority of the community. While official statements on the episcopacy often make appeal to the mission which the Twelve received from Jesus, it is somewhat ironical that this group is representative in the first place of the eschatological fellowship of the community formed in Jesus Christ. While Luke designates them as apostles, Matthew speaks of them as disciples. As a group they represent what it means to receive the message of the kingdom in Jesus Christ, what it means to follow his teaching, and what it means to live as a community, united in the hearing of the word and the celebration of the Supper. As they are the witnesses of Christ's ministry, death and resurrection, they are sent out as apostles to preach the good news, but even in this they are models for all those who believe in him.

Ministries which emerge in such a community have to be seen in their relation to God, to Christ, to the Spirit, and to the building up of the body of the church as a living witness to the kingdom of God in the world. The needs of the church and of its mission are what determine ministry. Ministry, then, comes from the Holy Spirit and is a particpation in the *diakonia* of Jesus Christ, and by that same token a sharing in his power to heal and to save. It has to be integrated into a church which finds in the twelve disciples a model of those who share in the messianic kingdom of God's blessings.

The most striking evidence of a plurality of services is found in Saint Paul, when he compares the church to a body: "God has appointed in the church first apostles, second prophets, third teachers, then workers of miracles, then healers, helpers, administrators, speakers in various tongues" (1 Corinthians 12.28). This is borne out by other parts of the New Testament, which refer to one or other of these ministries. It is also Paul who draws attention to the need for discernment and to the need for organization or ordering of ministries. It is the service and edification of the community which counts, not the glory of the one who receives the gift (cf. 1 Corinthians 14.5, 12, 19, 25, 26).

The charismatic origin and nature of service in the church is a factor to be kept in mind from the reading of the New Testament. There is first of all a rather prosaic, if necessary, way in which this is to be understood. There is no call, that is, that does not derive from the Spirit, and those called in the external forum of the church are promised the gifts of the Spirit for the exercise of their ministry. This is an attitude that the church takes up when she has worked out the distinctions of ministry and written the canons which ascribe function to specific bodies or orders, and it is an attitude which has a legitimate foundation in the New Testament. Since, however, it could be thought to imply too much about the origins and structures of certain forms of ministry, it is necessary to complete it with another way in which the proposition can be understood. This second way relies more on the persuasion that in Christ there are no official limits to the outpouring of the Spirit. The Spirit blows both where and how he wills, so that it is the free gift of the Spirit which determines the nature of the ministry to be conferred, as well as the person to be gifted with it. From such an understanding of the charismatic, it follows that unexpected services may arise at any time. It also follows that breaches may be created in the firm walls of canonical and theological formulations which restrict ministry by imposing specific forms and conditions. It is one thing for the church to stress that the call of the Spirit is necessary in order that a person be fitted to take up the ministries which she herself has already defined. It is another thing for the church to recognize that the call of the Spirit may sometimes transcend her definitions. It is at this stage that the church must use her powers of discernment to determine whether or not a given ministry that claims to possess the charism of the Spirit is truly consonant with the New Testament promises and criteria.

The charismatic view of ministry is too often related principally to its external manifestations. Perhaps this is in part due to the scholastic distinction between *gratia gratis data* and *gratia gratum faciens*. This seemed to imply that God's gifts for the service of others could be given to persons not otherwise in possession of the Spirit, or not much influenced in their personal lives by the Spirit. The power to prophesy, to speak in tongues, or to heal could thus be possessed by less likely Christians. There are no doubt times when such a distinction has a purpose, but it would seem that it is necessary as a general rule to build a stronger affinity between the charisms which serve the church and the charismatic's own inner possession of the gift of the Spirit.

This is a Pauline sense of charism. The Spirit gives to the one to whom he comes a knowledge of the mystery of Christ, as he also teaches compassion and teaches how to pray. It is on this basis that a person learns how to speak the word, how to comfort, how to lead, or how to heal. Basil of Caesarea in his treatise on the Holy Spirit has a clear grasp of this sense of charism. Basil felt that all gifts and all services flowed from the inner light of the Spirit which permitted the person gifted to behold and contemplate the mystery of the Father revealed in the image of the Son. From this there flows, he said, the knowledge of mystery, the gift of prophecy and of healing, and all other gifts, and finally godlikeness.[2]

This understanding of charism and service is the reason why the model of discipleship is one of the foremost models of ministry. The two coincide perfectly in the Twelve, and they manifest for ongoing ages the unity between the following of Christ and the apostolate. This is not merely because a good disciple makes a better apostle, but because the call to apostolate or other types of service is identical with discipleship. In the Twelve there is one of the primary images or figures of the kingdom to be found in the New Testament. Their table-fellowship with Jesus is the ground of their position in the church. This is not a purely personal quality belonging to the twelve persons, called Andrew, Peter, John, and so forth. Rather in this call to table-fellowship with the Christ they are the image of the new people, and this intimacy of discipleship and bond is at the same time the reason why they are sent as apostles or called upon to share the power and service of Jesus Christ. Instead of using the Twelve only as a model for hierarchy, they have to be allowed to stand as a model for every Christian service, in its radical discipleship and in its apostolic call.

Naturally enough, this ties in with what Paul has to say about the discernment of spirits. The spirits which represent the values and effects of the beatitudes are the ones to be judged authentic. It is really impossible to think of anyone possessing the Spirit without being called to serve a sister or a brother, and those who lay claim to gifts of service will best be judged by their fidelity to Jesus Christ and to his message, and by the way in which their service leads to fellowship.

As far as specific gifts are concerned, there is more in the New Testament about service to the word than there is about worship. Ministries of the word are quite varied, but there is no suggestion that they are limited to any office or any group of persons. There are the three principal ministries of apostle, prophet and teacher, and there are also such services as singing or praying in ways prompted by the Spirit. Not even the first three are limited to officeholders, it would seem.

Because of their fundamental nature in a community which is built on the word, it is not surprising to note that these word ministries are the ones which stand most in need of discernment and of recognition by the church. This is probably why they so easily became limited to officeholders, or even conferred with a call to office, but this is not necessarily in their nature. In short, a knowledge of the New Testament makes it possible to distinguish between the call to an appropriate ministry of the word which comes from a personal gift of the Spirit, the reception of this ministry by the community, and the control of word ministries which in due time went with hierarchical office. Whatever the necessity of the forms of apostolic authority which later developed in the church, and there is no intention here of denying that need, the New Testament does not permit the church to confine the service of the word to members of the hierarchy. On the contrary, it suggests that it would be well for the church to recognize and to welcome the many gifts of word possessed within the community.

Healing, comforting, the service to the widow and the orphan, and other similar services are likewise gifts of the Spirit and ministries to the Church. They too are subject to some kind of ordering, as is especially evident in the case of the seven men called to minister at table (Acts 6). The important thing to note about them here is that they come from discipleship and possession of the Spirit, or from the outflow of a person's following of and adherence to Jesus Christ. Often enough, indeed, healing is the sign which accompanies preaching the word, and the service to the widow and the orphan is mentioned by James (1.27) as the basis of true charity. None of these gifts, therefore, not even healing, ought to be seen as something esoteric or divorced from personal faith and discipleship. They are related to the perception of the mystery of Christ which comes with the gift of the Spirit. They suppose the ability to relate certain features of the human condition, such as illness or sorrow or poverty, to the mystery of Christ, to see them in the light of the love of God made known in him.

In view of the questions raised today about instituting ministries, it is natural enough to ask whether we have anything to learn from the New Testament on this count. We cannot expect to find a direct answer to our question, but some food for thought there may well be. First of all, however, we have to purge our minds of the tendency to connect the laying-on of hands always and everywhere with ordination as we now know it. A certain number of texts do connect the laying-on of hands with ministry, but what the connection is requires some thought.[3] The laying-on of hands narrated in Acts 6 has to be read as an act of investiture with office, for here the seven are appointed by the apostles to waiting on tables. In Acts 13.3 it is a gesture whereby the community sends two of its members, already known for their charism and for their apostolate, on a mission to preach. The same gesture, mentioned in the Pastoral Letters (1 Timothy 4.14; 2 Timothy 1.6), apparently owes much to its Jewish origins and signifies that the recipient becomes an elder in the church.[4]

There is something indubitably fluid about this gesture which prevents us from identifying it exclusively with an ordination to office in the church or with a transmission of power or authority. It is true that in later centuries the laying-on of hands became the definite act of ordination to liturgical ministry. That is not the case in the New Testament accounts mentioned above. Nor indeed do they have any one significance, beyond their common reference to a ministry. In each case, the community expresses itself in relation to this ministry. In Acts 6, the laying-on of hands is to confer a charge; in the Pastoral Letters it confers a status and stirs its charisms "into flame"; in Acts 13 it is an affirmation of gifts already possessed, together with the sending on a particular mission.

Many of these elements have been taken up into the sacrament of order and made to center on the sacrament of the altar. However, the action described in the New Testament seems to have other potentialities. The ministry inferred (or conferred) is not liturgical, but it is either a service of the word or a service to the common life. The part of the community and its spokesmen is as much a recognition as it is a conferring of gifts for ministry. The New Testament texts in question speak of the commissioning to ministries other than the liturgical. This might suggest to us that while the sacrament of order, as it historically developed, is to be constantly connected with the liturgy as pivotal point, the laying-on of hands might be used in a blessing relating to other types of ministry which do not involve a liturgical ministry.

Whether or not it is good to resurrect a laying-on of hands distinct from the sacrament of order and used in conjunction with other ministries, I do not at this stage wish to say. What I am inferring is that the New Testament seems to indicate the possibility of a community inducting persons into office, or sending them on a mission through a laying-on of hands that is not an ordination. We saw that from the third to the fifth centuries, the laying-on of hands came to be reserved to the higher liturgical ministries, and at the same time served to bring a whole network of ministries under the monopoly of the orders of bishop, presbyter and deacon. As things evolved in the east, even lesser orders like that of reader and subdeacon were made part of the priesthood by the laying-on of hands. In the west, every type of particular institution became an "ordination," and thus was made part of the higher ministries. The few New Testament texts mentioned above suggest an order of things prior to this development, one wherein the laying-on of hands had a more fluid meaning and where not all blessing by the community had to be connected with liturgical office.

CHRIST, KINGDOM, MINISTRY

Whatever is said about ministries brings us back to conceptions of the church and its basic ministeriality. Individual ministries are determined by the self-image of the community and by its corresponding sense of mission. This is in effect a more fundamental cause or source of diversity in ministry than is the diversity of charisms or gifts.

One can reflect on the fact that the church originated in Jesus' proclamation of the kingdom of God and in the church's identification of that kingdom with the person of Jesus. There is a diversity of christologies which stem from the images and concepts of how the kingdom is fulfilled in him. There is a corresponding difference in ecclesiologies, because of the church's identification with the kingdom as it comes in him. To each way of conceiving Christ and the church there corresponds a unique way of conceiving the ministry. Discovering this diversity in the pre-New Testament and New Testament era, as exegetical studies now allow us to do, is a way of coming to terms with the inevitable diversity of our own era. It does not give us a set of patterns to follow, but it does give rise to thought and some criteria for discernment.

New Testament studies on the reign and kingdom of God, and on the relation of christology to this, are complex, but some trends can be noted.[7] It is agreed generally that the preaching of Jesus proclaimed the coming of God's reign, as it is also generally agreed that the disciples and early Christian communities identified that coming with the person of Jesus himself and with how God had intervened in human history in the events of his ministry, death, and resurrection. How they perceived this connection, however, differed. Much of the New Testament literature shows how different communities, in different external and internal circumstances, developed in a more or less organic fashion their beliefs in the advent of God's reign, in Jesus Christ himself, and in the nature of the church as Christ's discipleship, caught up in the coming of God's reign.

In recent times, it has been pointed out frequently that the metaphors of kingdom, reign, or rule of God are not primarily spatial and do not refer to an exact order of things that God is to bring about in this world. They designate primarily God's saving activity, the divine exercise of lordship, which is the bringing about of justice, peace, and life in victory over the powers of sin and death. Despite this insist-

ence on the divine action designated by the metaphor, however, it has to be admitted that in the New
Testament there is some localization of the reign and
some measure of identification of the kingdom with
the church, differing from book to book.[8] As with all
attempts at a historical reconstruction of the life and
words of Jesus, there are different ideas and opinions
among scholars as to the exact nature and tenor of Jesus's own proclamation of God's reign. The point is
not directly pertinent to our concern with ministry in
the church, where the task is rather to see in the New
Testament literature how different communities or
churches developed their ideas about the reign or
kingdom of God, together with their beliefs about Jesus Christ as God's messenger, and about his eschatological relevance.

Although some scholars are dubious about the uses
made of Mark's Gospel and its sources, given the absence of any identifiable body of literature to mark
those sources, it is nonetheless worth noting some of
the conclusions of Edward Schillebeeckx and Norman
Perrin about the connection between church and
God's reign that this study reveals.[9] Schillebeeckx lo-
cates an initial christological faith in the Q community of New Testament exegetes. This faith's special
characteristic is that it finds in Jesus the coming
judge of the world, meaning salvation for some and
condemnation for others. As it is the mark of this belief to connect Jesus with the apocalyptic expectations
of Jewish communities in the intertestamental period,
the community that holds such belief is quite naturally one that is enthusiastic about the coming parousia. The renunciation of possessions, neglect of
earthly affairs, unconditional trust in God, and a special concern for the hungry and the poor are characteristic of the community. Schillebeeckx finds that the
beliefs of the pre-New-Testament community are
completed in Mark's Gospel in the sense that the

Gospel's author is more aware of the period of trial and suffering that precedes the parousia. The Gospel nonetheless retains a strong sense of the parousia's imminence and so is equally unconcerned about the things of the world, and about foreseeing what belongs to a historical future of the kingdom and its followers in the world.

Adopting a similar point of view, Perrin states: "The Christian apocalypticist despaired of the world and its history, but had faith in God who was about to change it."[10] As far as the life of the community is concerned, Perrin notes the accent on obedience to the teaching of Jesus about the kingdom. Power and authority belong to those who can endure suffering in Jesus's name. The principal ministry is to preach the word of the coming divine rule and judgment, and to help believers endure to the end, ready to face the reversal of worldly expectations that this entails.

Whatever the accuracy of this kind of historical reconstruction, one cannot deny the influence on early Christian belief of apocalyptic vision, nor its periodic fascination for the Christian imagination, especially in time of catastrophe. Negatively, this can lead to a ready condemnation of all the things of this world, a naive expectation for the overthrow of the powers of evil, and a lack of involvement in the positive attempts to bring about an order of justice and peace. As properly observed, Old Testament and New Testament apocalyptic means not only destruction but the advent of a new reality, not only condemnation but salvation.[11] What is negative in the apocalyptic vision of the cosmos can be paradoxically positive, however, since it loosens the hold on what is secure and in place, and readies the spirit to accept innovation. Theocracy, priestly rule, or rabbinic interpretation of the law was necessarily shaken in the minds of those who looked to Jesus as God's judgment and advent.

Likewise, in any age where there has been a hardening of institutional factors in the life of the church or of the state, a Christian reading of the eschatological elements in the New Testament is a reminder of the discontinuous continuity of God's dealings with the world. As Johannes Metz has put it, the apocalyptic sting in the message of Jesus transmitted through the Gospel is a reminder of the discontinuity in all human enterprise, inclusive of the religious.[12] A ministry of witness and proclamation must inevitably integrate this element of Christ's mystery.

The picture of the church that emerges from Luke-Acts is dominated by the sending of the Spirit of Jesus to the disciples, and its continuous presence in the church. Since the Pentecostal message is that the Spirit is poured out upon all, this leads to a charismatic perception of Christian life and of community ministry, which is quite interestingly connected by the author with an emergence of structures of leadership and service. More fundamental in the writer's vision is the relation between Jesus and the disciple that results from the gift of the Spirit: "the presence of the spirit of Jesus in the world, linking the believer with the sacred life and sacred time of Jesus, empowers the believer to exhibit the same quality of life in the world that Jesus did. This is borne out in the heroes of the Church whose lives paralleled Jesus in many respect."[13]

This theology seems to incorporate a perception of Jesus himself as a divine hero, or as the divine wisdom, who by an act of divine condescension and humility comes into the world, so that both Jesus and the apostles appear to some extent as mystagogues who initiate believers into the wisdom that is present and hidden in Jesus.[14] Since Luke-Acts places much stress on Jesus's mission to the poor and on the poverty of his life as the very condition of his power, one is not surprised to see the important place that this

112

has in the ministry of the apostles and in what is expected of the believer or disciple. The whole future of the church is to be guided by the Spirit and is to be a witness to the power of the Spirit of Jesus in bringing about a new creation that will touch all people.

Some of the tendencies to see Jesus as either eschatological prophet or divine wisdom found eventual expression in the view of revelation and salvation that is found in Matthew's Gospel. The community reflected in this Gospel faced the delay of the parousia by giving more attention to the ethical teaching of Jesus, believed to fulfill the law and the prophets. In Matthew, there is the conviction that there is a correspondence between the revealed truth of Jesus's teaching and the life experience of Christians in the world. It is through this teaching that the glorified Jesus remains in the church and in the world.[15] This means, of course, that the church gives much attention to the ministry and to the authority of teaching. For all that, the Matthean community is one in which the power of the teacher comes from discipleship, while regulation of community life rests with the community as such, this being in no way contrary to the necessity of leadership.

It is also in Matthew's Gospel that we note the tendency to localize God's reign and kingdom, with a partial identification between church and kingdom.[16] Apparently, the author wanted to point out that there was a definite place or group in which the teaching of Jesus was both followed and taught, and that this could be identified both by the example of those who belonged in it and by its assimilation of certain structures of authoritative teaching, which contrasted with the ways of the scribes and the Pharisees. This helped to establish both continuity with the law and the prophets, and the openness of the Gospel and the promise of the kingdom to the gentiles. Ironically, the gospel that sought to open the minds of certain Jews

113

and Judeo-Christians to the flexibility of God's ways could be used in later centuries as an instrument of Christian rigidity, because of the spatialization of the metaphor of God's reign.

The identification between church and kingdom was pushed further by the communities represented in the deutero-Pauline letters to the Colossians and Ephesians, which also embody a cosmic christology.[17] The identification between church and kingdom is due to the glorification of Christ and to the identification of the church as his body. All principalities and powers are subjected to Christ, who is the head of the church, and the body is intended to envelope all cosmic reality. Thus the Christians of these churches were offered a cosmic vision that coincided with the sense of their identity as the body of Christ in the world, and that allowed them to have a perception of the church as a global body, of which each local community was a living cell.

By way of contrast with Matthew and with these deutero-Pauline epistles, the metaphors of reign and kingdom do not occur at all in John's Gospel. This is not to say that the writer is ignorant of the metaphor of the kingdom. What he has done is to associate all the images that in Old Testament and in other New Testament writings are predicated of the reign of kingdom of God with Jesus himself.[18] This has a double effect. First of all, it says very strongly that God's advent and saving activity are to be identified with Jesus Christ. Secondly, it says equally strongly that the disciples are bound personally and intimately to him as the source of life, and that the church is the community of such persons. All are taught by the Spirit, all give witness to Christ, all are nourished by the gift of his life. Naturally, this vision of the church does not give much place to church structures or to positions of authority, since it is the call and mission of each and every disciple that is brought to the fore.

114

The cosmic vision of the writer merges with his vision of the church, since what is awaited is the resurrection of all flesh, to partake of the life of the risen and glorious Christ.[19]

At the end of his second christological volume, Edward Schillebeeckx, having dealt with the canonical literature, expresses the conviction that the life of the Christian community, as it lives in the world, can be said to be built upon a quadruple structure.[20] Salvation comes when God works out his historical plan with humankind: his name indicates his solidarity with his people. The essence of that history enters into our experience in the person and life of Jesus. Consequently, our history is to follow Jesus. Though this is common to all the canonical writings, Schillebeeckx finds it more sharply expressed in John's Gospel than elsewhere, for in that work the blending of the events of Jesus' life with the history of the believing community is so clear that it serves as a model for all time.[21] Finally and fourthly, he finds that life with Christ in God is to be lived as a history without historical term. That is to say, that the eschatological perspective of Christian belief is totally centered on life with God, and so does not mean that we can determine the when and how of the consummation.

In reaching these conclusions about the common structures of Christian life, Schillebeeckx wants to indicate the direction that belief in Christ will take, and he is persuaded that at any time in history human beings can live out this New Testament belief and teaching about Christ. This is not, of course, to deny plurality, which would be a direct contradiction of the author's entire enterprise, which is to wrestle from the New Testament christological and soteriological possibilities not fully appreciated in the course of the history which has been hitherto lived. Plurality remains, coming both from the situation to be faced and from the New Testament canon itself. The common structure, then, is a sign of unity in diversity, rather than a way of suppressing diversity.

As already stated, my intention in this elaboration on New Testament christology and ecclesiology has been to make the point that different perceptions of God's kingdom will mean different ways of ministering. As a kind of summary, one could say that in the vision of the kingdom as imminent judgment there is rooted a ministry which prepares the world for judgment; that in the vision of the kingdom as the work of Christ for the poor and the outcast in the power of the Spirit, there is rooted a ministry which is charismatic and oriented to service; that in the vision of the kingdom as that which comes in the cross of Jesus, there is rooted a ministry which contests the folly of this world and preaches freedom as the Father's gift in the face of evil; that in the vision of the kingdom which sees it as the influence of Jesus' teaching on the world, there is rooted a ministry which propounds and elaborates on that teaching as the norm for godlike conduct.

What does all of this have to say to the present question of lay ministry in the church? It seems to indicate that the main issue is not that of the respective roles of ordained and nonordained, since it is always necessary to go to the self-understanding of the community to know what its ministry will be. It is on the basis of the church's will to proclaim the kingdom in life, in word, and in deed that the concept of ministry applicable to all the baptized has to be developed, and the various questions relative to the division of responsibilities and powers pondered.

Certainly I am not proposing a one-to-one equation between pre-New Testament and New Testament ways of imaging the kingdom and contemporary ways of doing so. The comparison is rougher than that, since modern communities seem to pull together different sets of images, titles, and symbols of Christ than did any given tradition within the canonical books. The fact is that the kingdom is presented in such diverse ways in New Testament times that no perfect synthesis has ever been achieved. As a result there are different kinds of Christian communities, depending on the community's view of how it is to work for the spread of the kingdom, since a people finds its meaning and identity in a cluster of images, symbols and stories beneath the level of institution and practice.

Often it is a greater openness to culture and to sociopolitical realities which occasions new questions and thus new styles in the way of remembering Christ and being community. One good example is a tendency now found in African churches. Many of these churches are beyond the stage of simply observing that western ways of choosing priests and western attitudes toward celibacy ought not to dominate questions of ministry in Africa. They are even beyond the point of arguing the necessity of basic Christian community as structure. Though they still have to fight these points, they are seen as only a small step toward changing ministry. What is more serious is that African churches have to accept different kinds of question and concern. Ministry is concerned about relations with the invisible world, in which Christ's dominion over principalities and powers, and his power to free those who live in the world of spirits, becomes important. Ministry has to mediate between two worlds and reconcile the present with the past of the ancestors and with their living spirits. Mediation between the living and the dead, and a ministry which is directed to bodily and psychic health along the lines of Jesus' healing of the possessed, are some of the prominent functions necessary to these churches. In their desire to share the gospel they find themselves evoking gospel images of Christ which the west does not now consider to any great extent. As Bishop Sanon of Upper Volta has stated,

"the actual experience of the communities and their actual questions about the role of the Spirit and spirits in the world, communication between the visible and invisible worlds, and the material and eschatological dimensions of man and life, will be the major topics of the process of research and discovery."[22]

One could look for another kind of Christian experience in the churches of Latin America. There, the kind of mysticism which is associated with John's Gospel becomes the foundation for political commitment. As Segundo Galilea writes, Christians in Latin America

"see salvation as tied to temporal and political commitments, although they do not reduce it to temporal liberation. They give great importance to the praxis of liberation and discover in prayer the guarantee that evangelical values preside over that praxis. Their commitment itself, at times a very radical one, has led them in many cases to bring their faith to a high degree of Christian mysticism."[23]

A kind of practical christology derives from this commitment, one which lays great emphasis on the Son's identification through his *kenosis* with the poor. Because of the Son's communion with the Father, the divinity itself is known in this self-emptying of Christ, in this commitment of the Son to the poor and oppressed. The church's communion with the Son, the Son's union with his Father and the mission which he receives from the Father are revealed in the church's commitment to the poor. It is this dedication to the service of the poor, and the church's identity as the household of the poor, which serve as the criteria for the discernment of ministries.[24]

In highly technological societies, people are impressed by still other images of Christ and of the kingdom. As a result, the question of ministry is put in different ways. For those who face the problem of being both modern and Christian, the church's mediation is sought out in terms of a service in the name of Christ to true human freedom in a world of "progress." This can even take the form of a kind of neoconservatism which is willing to change the structure of the church in favor of a fuller diversity in ministry, provided this supports the church's claim to possess the one truth of revelation in Jesus Christ. Community ties are strengthened and the teaching of Jesus and of his church are looked to as the one norm of human conduct. An example of this kind of Christian experience is found in the neo-catechumenal movement, which originated in Spain and has spread to many countries.[25] The intention of the movement is to renew Christian community by giving those baptized in infancy an adult experience of community, based on the catechumenate of the fourth and fifth century church. This model is taken because of the similarity between Christians in the world today and Christians of that era. At that time, the church flourished because it had found its peace with the empire, but its members succumbed all too easily to human blandishments. A strong adult catechumenal experience was therefore necessary. It is the persuasion of the founders of the neo-catechumenal movement that today many baptized Christians are more at one with the secular world than they are at one with the faith of Christ. Hence, renewal postulates a strong catechumenal experience. The movement embraces a strong Pauline opposition between the wisdom of the cross and the folly of the world. There is "no philosophy, politics or science by which mankind can be saved."[26] It is only in the truth of Christ's cross that God's love saves humanity. Within this model of community experience, a considerable development of ministries takes place, allowing for the presbyter-pastors, local catechists, itinerant preachers (lay), singers, readers, doorkeepers, widows and teachers.[27]

These are but some examples of how community self-identity decides the way ministry develops, and of how fundamental it is to determine the nature of the community Christian experience before the question of ministries can be discussed. A thorough typology of present-day communities would be a large task. These few examples serve merely to illustrate the major lesson about ministry which we learn from reading the New Testament, namely, that the shape of the community experience of the kingdom and the consequent shape of its own identity is far more fundamental that mere rules and regulations, names and titles.

Ministeriality is a quality of the church community as a unit or a body, before it is a predicate of any of its members. The fundamental principle for an understanding and a structuring of ministry is that the church is the sacrament of God's kingdom in the world, a living presence which must deal with temporal questions. How the church sees itself in relation to these questions determines the ministeriality of the community. To predicate secular concerns of the laity and divine or strictly religious concerns of the clergy may be a useful rule of thumb in some situations, but it hardly serves as a basic theological proposition. To offer it as such would be a practical denial of the New Testament's way of identifying the church with the experience of the kingdom of God. Today also we have to look to the community's experience of Christ and of the kingdom in order to discern the charisms and ministries of the church. The first task is to identify the reality of Christian community, since this cannot be presumed to be identical with the canonical entity called diocese or parish.

NOTES

1. For a synthesis of the question, see B. Cooke, *Ministry to Word and Sacrament* (Fortress Press, Philadelphia 1976), chaps. 1, 8, 15, 20, 27. On the development of the notion of "twelve apostles," see W. Schmithals, *The Office of Apostle in the Early Church*, translated by John F. Steely (Abingdon Press, Nashville 1979). The Twelve, apostle, and twelve apostles are three distinct concepts.

2. Basil of Caesarea, *Treatise on the Holy Spirit*, chap. 9, 23, A Select Library of Nicene and Post-Nicene Fathers of the Christian Church, Second Series, vol. 8 (The Christian Literature Company, New York 1895), pp. 15-16.

3. See J.-K. Parrett, "The Laying-on of Hands in the New Testament," *Expository Times* 80 (1969) 210-214; E. Lohse, "Cheir," *TWNT* 8 (1966) 161-162; E. J. Kilmartin, "Ministère et Ordination dans l'Eglise chrétienne primitive," *La Maison-Dieu* 138 (1979) 49-92.

4. See J. Delorme, "Diversité et Unité des Ministères d'après le Nouveau Testament," in *Le Ministère et les Ministères selon le Nouveau Testament*, sous la direction de Jean Delorme (Editions du Seuil, Paris 1974) 340.

5. *Lumen gentium* 28 and *Presbyterorum ordinis* 2.

6. *Presbyterorum ordinis* 5.

7. On the reign and kingdom of God, cf. Norman Perrin, *Jesus and the Language of the Kingdom* (Fortress Press, Philadelphia 1976); Rudolf Schnackenburg, *God's Rule and Kingdom* (Herder & Herder, New York 1967).

8. Cf. Raymond Brown, *The Churches the Apostles Left Behind* (Paulist, New York 1984) 51.

9. In his work *Jesus: An Experiment in Christology*, translated by H. Hoskins (Seabury Press, New York 1979), Edward Schillebeeckx points to the relation between christology, ecclesiology, and notions of the kingdom in the different books of the New Testament. Cf. also Norman Perrin, *The New Testament: An Introduction* (Harcourt Brace Jovanovich, New York 1974).

10. Perrin, *The New Testament* 306.

11. Amos N. Wilder, *Jesus' Parables and the War of Myths: Essays on Imagination in the Scriptures*, edited, with a preface, by James Breech (Fortress Press, Philadelphia 1982) 153–168.

12. Johann Baptist Metz, *Faith in History and Society: Toward a Practical Fundamental Theology*, translated by David Smith (Seabury Press, New York 1980) 73f.

13. Perrin, *The New Testament* 307.

14. Schillebeeckx, *Jesus* 429–432.

15. Perrin, *The New Testament* 307.

16. Brown, *The Churches* 124–145.

17. Brown 47–60.

18. Brown 87.

19. Brown 95–97.

20. Edward Schillebeeckx, *Christ: The Experience of Jesus as Lord* (Seabury Press, New York 1980) 629–644.

21. Schillebeeckx, *Christus*, 622.

22. A. Titianme Sanon, "The New Gospel in a Millenarian Church," in *The Churches of Africa: Future Prospects*, C. Geffré and B. Luneau, eds., *Concilium* 106 (Seabury Press, New York 1977), 92.

23. Segundo Galilea, "Liberation as an Encounter with Politics and Contemplation," in *The Mystical and Political Dimension of the Christian Faith*, C. Geffré and G. Guttierez, eds., *Concilium* 96 (Herder & Herder, New York 1974), 22.

24. See J. Sobrino, "Following Jesus as Discernment," in *Discernment of the Spirit and of Spirits*, C. Floristan and C. Duquoc, eds., *Concilium* 119 (Seabury Press, New York 1979), 14-24.

25. See G. Zevini, "The Christian Initiation of Adults into the Neo-Catechumenal Community," in *Structures of Initiation in Crisis*, L. Maldonado and D. Power, eds., *Concilium* 122 (Seabury Press, New York 1979), 65-74.

26. Zevini 72.

27. See Zevini 70.

The Ongoing Present

Chapter Five

From the Edges to the Center

In the preceding chapters of this work, lay ministry has been investigated on the current scene, in the context of early church history, and in the light of the New Testament. A phenomenology of ministries and services, a theology of the church, and a theology of vocation are all involved in the issue. Is it now possible to offer a theological viewpoint of some consistency on ministries, their origin and their recognition? Can a key idea be found around which different items may be arranged and unified?

THE PHENOMENON IN THE LIGHT OF HISTORY

The most remarkable thing about the development of ministries in today's churches is the manner of their relation to church renewal. One might be tempted to say that where there are enough ministries and good ministers, the renewal of the church will follow. It is in this sense that prayers are often offered for vocations to the religious life or presbyterate. Today, however, what is happening is of the reverse order: where there is a renewal of community life, then a variety of ministries spring up. A vital grass-roots renewal is in many places giving rise to more abundant and more varied services.

The revitalization starts with the meeting of persons in a community of faith and in a shared desire to live a common life based on this faith. A new interest in the Bible, a willingness to share the faith with one another, the will to live and support one another as sister and brother, the move to stand as a body in the face of needs and social issues, are the factors which converge to constitute a fresh sense of Christian fellowship. It is usually within such communities of faith that individual persons discover their call to service in the Spirit, the charisms whereby they work in the community or share its evangelical mission. There are indeed occasions when a prophet appears to stir up consciences, as a revivalist asks for a pledge to Christ, but the renewal starts in earnest only as a community enterprise.

To say this is not to reduce all phenomena of Christian community to a common denominator. This would be to neglect the fact that the movement to more intense community, together with its resurgence of ministries, is multicolored. While there are many communities, they are of quite different temper and their relation to the parent church is not always the same. One need only think of such different things as basic Christian communities of the Latin American type, neo-catechumenal communities, marriage encounter communities, or interconfessional communities to realize this diversity. Only by taking these few examples, one is brought up against the realization that the movement embodies quite different ways of relating to the hierarchy, as well as different ways of envisaging the relation of the church to the secular world or to other religions. The mixture of the ritual, the mystical, and the prophetic certainly has no fixed standards.

Varied as the movement may be, it is striking to note how much it changes the issue of ministries. Not since apostolic times has a grass-roots revival been allowed to determine or influence the shape of ministry in the way that many of these communities propose to do either by implication or by explicit demand. In the past history of the church, grass-roots revival has sometimes been at odds with the episcopacy; at other times it has been integrated into the church institution in the form, for example, of a religious order. Today, the thrust is for the community to remain distinctively lay, distinctly grass-roots, by taking the common responsibility and mission of the people as starting point. While it does not threaten to wipe out the sacrament of order, it places it in another perspective, one which makes it clearly auxiliary to the common mission rather than determinative of it and its modalities.

Pluralism in the image and structure of ministry is an inevitable feature of church life. The proper place for a discernment and approval of ministries is within local or particular communities of the baptized. This would be only naive idealism if we did not face the fact that the position of many of the baptized today is highly ambiguous. Many adhere to the church as an institution, one which satisfies their religious needs and dictates their religious duties. Others, while having been baptized into it, in religious practice and moral code adhere to a set of popular beliefs which are dubiously Christian or flatly syncretistic. To state that the call to mission is grounded in baptism under such circumstances is to make a purely fabulous statement and to ignore the facts of the matter.

Unfortunately, the question of ministry, lay and ordained, often gets mixed up with the effort to keep numbers and serve in some way the religious needs of the uncommitted. When the ecclesiastical unit considered is that of the baptized in a given parish or diocese, or even the number of church-goers, then it inevitably becomes a matter of the clergy acquiring a few willing helpers to provide some auxiliary services, or else the camouflage of lay participation which is sewn together by increasing the number of lay readers and extraordinary ministers of communion.[1]

A good part of the difficulty which is encountered in renewing lay ministries is due to the fact that too much is made of baptism as a rite or ceremony, not enough of the greater realities of initiation into a faith community. On the opposite side, and much linked with this tendency, too much is made of the priesthood or sacrament of order. One of the reasons for this is the practical one that not much can be expected from the casually baptized. Another reason is that order itself has been mysticized as the source of power and authority almost without considering the faith and charism of the person ordained. The theory developed in the Middle Ages, that the validity of the sacraments did not depend on the worthiness of the minister, tended to place his worthiness in a subordinate position and has become almost a theological maxim. With regard to both baptism and order it is possible to speak of a practical breakdown of the sacramental system. It is a breakdown which can be dealt with only by a demysticization or demythologization of these two sacraments as part of a process to retrieve their true significance for the church and its mission.

This process has to take place within a serious community context. It is by taking faith communities in earnest as bodies wherein the single members possess the Spirit and his gifts, and all are together responsible, that a revitalization of ministries comes about. This does not suggest that order is unnecessary. Nor does the assertion mean that the power of the presbyter, or any other power for that matter, comes from the people, since all power in the church is from Christ and his Spirit. All I want to say is that in looking for the meaning of order in the church it is necessary to leave behind the theological and canonical system which had its point of departure in the hierarchy, and look instead to the reality of the unit which is the people of God in Christ, and locate grace and discernment in that body.

A NEW KEY?
In her book, *Philosophy in a New Key*, Suzanne Langer[2] remarks that the sign of the dawn of a new age is the

emergence of a key idea which seems to allow all reality to be perceived and shared in a new way. Many are inspired by this key idea and seek to gain entry into new fields, or to find new ways into old ones, while others, however, still go on working over the rubble of a failed or tiring system.

The primary expression of meaning and the most rudimentary expression of meaning is through symbol, and reality is transformed through symbolic usage. Can we actually retrieve the primary symbols of ministry, understanding them not only through the historical-critical method but by actually reading them as symbols? This would mean discovering their creative possibility and not merely the sources from which they derive or the original context in which they were used. We might then be able to express what is going on in the church at present through a creative use of these symbols, in such a way as to gain the kind of insight which leads to both understanding and action.

While in the New Testament the meaning of ministry was expressed through such symbolic words as *diakonia, exousia, charis,* and related to symbols of people, kingdom, and eschaton, these symbols have suffered sedimentation in the course of time. Sedimentation of a symbol occurs when the symbol is translated into a conceptual meaning or is made to support a definite juridical structure, and such a meaning is then the only one attached to the symbol. It then becomes more of a sign than a symbol, for it serves only as a reminder and does not evoke new inquiry or reflection. This happens constantly in liturgy and in creedal expression. For example, attention is focused on the symbols of bread and wine as signs that tell the community of Christ's presence, but the reasons why precisely bread and wine were chosen to evoke the meaning of the fellowship of the church in Christ, are often overlooked. For many, the water in baptism has significance only as a cleansing power, without reference to its evocation of the mystery of death and rebirth. Words significant of power are attached to the canonical structure of a diocese, to the detriment of the *pneuma* which they invoke.

Such a debilitation has taken place with the word *ministry* itself. For long centuries ministry was applied only to the work of the ordained members of the church, as this was spelt out in canonical and theological literature. The Second Vatican Council indeed did not go beyond this stage of usage, since it did not employ *ministry* when speaking of the activities of the laity. Sacralization of that reality to which the term is reserved imposes limitations on the way the word is used. To make a term univocal results in sacralizing its referent.

There is something inevitable and necessary about the process whereby the symbols and the symbolized are harmonized, but the harmony has at times to be broken in order to allow for further development. In the case of a symbol that has been in constant use, it is almost inevitable that it will undergo a long-term process of sacralization, desacralization of what has been sacralized, and resacralization of the evolved reality which results from the creative use of the symbol, such creative use being possible, of course, through an initial desacralization of the object to which it had become attached.

How did all of this occur in the case of ministry? In the original call of the Israelite people, there is no place for king or priest, since all power is invested in the prophet sent by God as leader and the people are themselves a royal priesthood. In time, however, the image of prophet lost some of its power which, in turn, was transferred to the king or the priest, who were chosen and appointed by God as his "sons." This also meant that the power of God which resided in the people was transferred to their appointed leaders, be they king or priest. The people's expectations came to be invested in

130

the hope of a new leadership which, combining the qualities of both king and priest, would forge them into a powerful nation.

The New Testament in effect both desacralized and re-sacralized the use of the images of priest, prophet and king. This it did firstly through its narrative and theology of the humble self-emptying and service of Jesus Christ, in whom these expectations are strangely fulfilled; secondly by proclaiming a general outpouring of the Spirit, which revived the image of the chosen people, the royal and prophetic priesthood. The power of God (*exousia*) came into the world in Jesus, but the *diákonos* is the new image of power, as are the disciples sent by Jesus to be his apostles; or the prophets who can speak the word of the kingdom to the people; or the charismatics who are given some share in the Spirit of Jesus Christ. If the image of the individual who is prophet, priest, or king had not been desacralized, this new sacralization of service through these images—which is totally dependent on the basic image of the royal and prophetic people, one in Christ and his Spirit—could not have taken place.

The early history of the church gives evidence that a resacralization took place, this time by sacralizing bishops and presbyters, by attaching to them particular images. By this process, the sacred media of word and sacrament, and the power to judge in Christ's name, with which the new people of God had been endowed, were absorbed into the authority of the clergy. Leadership and order and ritual are necessary to the church, and it seems a necessary part of the sacrament of order that the leadership or presidency of the church be sacramentally related through the eucharist to the *diakonia* of Jesus Christ and to the power of his Spirit. The sacralization of the authority of bishop and presbyter may also have been a historical or cultural necessity, but it is not an essential part of order, not something vital to the nature and ministry of the church.

In the last few decades, some desacralization of the office of bishop and presbyter has taken place. This not only does not threaten seriously the place of the sacrament of order in the church, but it is a necessity if the more basic symbol and reality of the service of God's people and the general outpouring of the Spirit are to be retrieved and allowed to revivify the sense of the mission of the whole body.

As already intimated, some desacralization of baptism is necessary lest the faith community be confused with the number of the baptized. With the fact that infant baptism became not only usual but normal (or normative), induction into the faith community receded into the background, and so did the celebration of the believing community. The value attached to baptism when it is validly administered, whatever the circumstances under which this is done, amounts to a sacralization of the rite. What needs to be taken into consideration is that baptism has its true meaning in the context of a community of faith.

Aidan Kavanagh in his work *The Shape of Baptism* trenchantly recalls that though infant baptism is without question legitimate and attested by tradition, it is not normal:

"The normal as defined by tradition is differentiated from the usual as defined by convention. The notion that infant baptism must be regarded as something less than normal cannot set easily with many Catholics, lay as well as clerical, who have never known anything else. But its abnormality does not require one to conclude that it is illegitimate: tradition clearly seems to know the baptism of infants from its beginning. But tradition with equal clarity does *not* know one thing often implied by the conventional frequency of infant baptism, namely, that baptism in infancy is the normal manner in which one becomes a Catholic Christian."[3]

The normal is better perceived in what the writer describes as the sequence found in New Testament accounts, when proclamation and conversion precede baptism in water and the Spirit. Under such circumstances the rite is an entry into a community "in which the gospel has begun to become praxis."[4] Whatever, therefore, be the situation of the person who is a candidate for baptism, whether child or adult, the context of a living faith community has to be verifiable before it is possible to speak of the sacrament as entry into the church. A theology of baptism which speaks only of the rite and fails to relate the rite to the reality of membership in the community is delusory.

It has been necessary to treat of the desacralization of the rite of ordination and of the desacralization of the rite of baptism in order to put the discussion of lay ministry into proper focus. On the one hand, the desacralization of the sacrament of order makes it possible to look to baptism for the foundation of the call to service and ministry in the church. On the other hand, the desacralization of baptismal practices makes it clear that this is done with the reality of the believing community in mind.

The theology of ministry, if it is to serve the renewal of its practice, needs to explain how baptism constitutes a call to share in the mission of the church, while at the same time making proper allowance for the sacrament of order. The symbol of the "holy people" is a good starting point for a theology which brings these two factors together in a harmonious fashion. The symbol stands out to best advantage when it is applied to the people who have been initiated into the church through baptism and gather together for the celebration of the eucharist. In its sacramental context it speaks of the eschatological community which shares in the mystery of the Lord's pasch and partakes of his holy table. It is a symbol which can integrate the images of covenant, kingdom, worship, mission, prophecy, and Spirit. It respects the richness of each of these images since of its nature it includes the idea of history. One cannot think of a people without thinking of its history, and each of the images mentioned above belongs to the history of the eschatological people. Rudolph Otto's statement of the mystery of the holy people is still powerful and evocative today. Writing of the numinous in the New Testament, he states:

"The 'kingdom' is just greatness and marvel absolute, the 'wholly other' 'heavenly' thing, set in contrast to the world of here and now, the 'mysterious' itself in its dual character as awe-compelling yet all-attracting, glimmering in an atmosphere of genuine 'religious awe.' As such, it sheds a color, a mood, a tone, upon whatever stands in relation to it, upon the men who proclaim it or prepare for it, upon the life and practice that are its precondition, upon the tidings of it, upon the congregation of those who await it and attain it. All is made into mystery—all, that is, becomes numinous. This is shown most strikingly in the name by which the company of the disciples call themselves collectively and each other individually, the numinous 'technical term' of *oi hágioi,* the holy ones or 'the saints.' It is manifest at once that this does not mean 'the morally perfect' people: it means the people who participate in the mystery of the final Day."[5]

In 1 Peter 2.9 this symbol of the "holy people" occurs together with those of the "royal priesthood" and "chosen people." The text is often used in ecclesiology as one in which the reality of the church is expressed quite comprehensively. The context in which it occurs is an exhortation to confidence in the blood of Christ and to conduct befitting those who have received redemption through such a price. The author is speaking of the mystery of election and of the perfection that is possible to those who believe. In that sense, the images of holy people and royal priesthood are addressed to the moral life. It would, however, be a mistake to think that this exhausts their meaning. Of their nature, they refer to a more ample mystery, to that which is the foundation of a good life. This is the mystery of the kingdom proclaimed in Jesus Christ and of the judgment of God given in that proclamation. The holiness of the people may be expressed in their moral conduct and in their worship, but it is something more basic than such action. It is their alliance with God in the mystery of his own being, the introduction into a reality which far transcends the human and the earthly even while being manifested in human form.

The images of the holy people and royal priesthood are frequently used to express that which is proper to baptismal initiation as distinct from ordination. Following this common usage, the Second Vatican Council in the Constitution on the Church distinguished between the priesthood of order and the priesthood of the laity,[6] going on to remark that there is not only a difference of degree but a difference of kind between these two. The use of the word "priesthood" in the conciliar text is, however, equivocal and consequently fails to address the question of the laity's call to mission and of the relation of this call to that of ordination. The equivocation comes from the fact that the text deliberately uses "priesthood" of baptism in order to express holiness of life, whereas it uses the same word of ordination in order to express ministry. Holiness of life and ministry are certainly distinct in kind. That, however, cannot prevent us from asking whether some call to ministry comes with baptism, and if so what is its relation to the call to ministry in ordination. Similarly, it does not prevent us from asking whether there is a due relationship between holiness of life and ministerial activity.

When the symbol of the holy people is related to the baptismal and eucharistic community, this evokes the doctrinal and theological tradition which speaks of the sacramental character given in baptism. In western writings this tradition has its foundation in the writings of Saint Augustine on baptism.[7] Augustine defended the practice of not repeating baptismal immersion once it had been properly administered and the Trinity had been invoked, even if this had been done outside the communion of the church. Not all the effects of baptism followed in such a case, and indeed the persons concerned could not be said to share the communion of the church in the Spirit until they were reconciled with it. However, according to Augustine, since the word of faith and the immersion expressed the mystery of Christ they brought the baptized person into an irrevocable relationship to the church and the rite could be looked upon as a mark or consecration that was permanent.

While Augustine developed these ideas to explain why baptism given by heretics was not to be repeated on their reconciliation, it is apparent that he spoke of a fundamental aspect of the membership of the church that is given through baptism. Consequently, it was later possible to develop his ideas further outside the context in which he had expressed them. Some recent studies on the sacramental character speak of it as the ecclesial effect of baptism, distinguishing this from the effect of personal sanctification.[8] The idea is not to separate the two effects but to show how they are organically related. Personal sanctification for a Christian comes about through insertion into the church and into the mystery of Christ, of which the church is itself a sacrament. One study[9] makes a connection between the western doctrine of sacramental character and the Greek teaching on sealing with the Holy Spirit. Whatever the niceties of historical study may say to this, it is a useful insight. What it says is that the gift of the Holy Spirit is the very basis of the mystery of the church and hence of all participation in its life and in its sacraments.

When the symbol of the holy people is taken in conjunction with this tradition on the sacramental character, it says to us that the holiness of God's people resides in the first instance in the stupendous fact that they are called by God as a people or church in whom the mystery of his kingdom is to be made manifest among the nations. The baptized are sacramentally immersed in this newness and mystery, so that as one body they drink of one Spirit. This ecclesial fact, this ingrafting into the kingdom through God's power, is the foundation of the people's holiness of life as it is also the foundation of their mission. Membership in the body, given in baptism and sustained at the eucharistic table, is the root of both discipleship and apostolate.

If this ecclesial reality is identified with the sealing with the Spirit which brings people into the sacramental and eschatological community, then it can be seen as the one ground of both grace and charism. Rather than explaining grace and charism as two quite distinct effects of the one sacrament, they can be explained as organically interrelated effects. In other words, there is an inseparable connection between what is generally called grace and what is generally called charism. They are both gifts of the Spirit, bestowed on those who share in the mystery of the church so that they can take full part in its life and mission. This is very well expressed in the tradition of the Greek Fathers, which speaks of the Holy Spirit as the illumination or enlightenment which makes knowledge of the Son and, thereby, a share in his divine life possible. Grace is a knowledge which gives knowledge of the Son and of the world in its dependence on the Son. Charism, or the gift of service, results from this enlightenment. Basil the Great expresses this harmony very adroitly in the following passage of his treatise on the Holy Spirit, referred to in Chapter Four:

"The Spirit, like the sun, will by the aid of thy purified eye show thee in himself the image of the invisible, and in the blessed spectacle of the image thou shalt behold the unspeakable beauty of the archetype. . . . Shining upon those that are cleansed from every spot, he makes them spiritual by fellowship with himself. Just as when a sunbeam falls on bright and transparent bodies, they themselves become brilliant too, and shed forth a fresh brightness from themselves, so souls wherein the Spirit dwells, illuminated by the Spirit, themselves become spiritual, and send forth their grace to others. Hence comes the foreknowledge of the future, understanding of mysteries, apprehension of what is hidden, distribution of charisms, the heavenly citizenship, a place in the chorus of angels, joy without end, abiding in God, the being made like God, and, highest of all, the being made God."[10]

Even though scholastic theology made the character of the sacrament of order the analogate for a consideration of the sacrament of baptism, historical studies make it clear that Augustine first worked out his understanding of the permanency of baptism. What theology today has to say about the character of order must be said by way of analogy with what is said about baptism. Indeed, the decree on presbyters of the Second Vatican Council reminds us that the sacrament of order and its call to ministry are founded on the sacraments of Christian initiation.[11] The link between ordination and baptism can be made, in keeping with early church tradition, through the charism of leadership. This charism, which the church looks for in its candidates for ordination, is one of the gifts of baptism. It is not indeed a gift possessed by all, since charisms are particular to the state, enlightenment and talent of each person. Where, however, it is found it is a gift which comes from the sealing of the Spirit in baptism and belongs to the mystery of the church which is celebrated in baptism and the eucharist. What the sacrament of order then does is to give the recipient a new role in the life of the church, and as principal expression of this, a special role in the celebration of the eucharist, where the mystery of the church is celebrated. His position becomes such that in the celebration of the Lord's Supper the relationship to Christ as founder and source of life, as well as the relationship to the community of the apostles and to the communion of all the churches, is expressed and served through his presidency. Because he is empowered to represent the church in this vital action, to represent to it its own very ground of being, we say that he is empowered to represent Christ.[12]

Presidency of community and presidency of the eucharist require the charism of leadership. They fittingly go together, and history suggests that it was one suited to the former who in fact assumed the latter. Currently theology very rightly teaches that in the sacrament of order one is simultaneously called to the triple ministry of liturgy, preaching and community presidency. While this allows for the harmony which must exist between these three ministries, it is now also possible to bring charism into this harmony by referring the charism of leadership back to baptism. The ministry of order is rooted in the call to mission and ministry which comes with being made a member of the holy people through the sacrament of baptism.

DISCERNMENT
The gifts of service which are the result of baptism and which develop through participation in the church's mystery are not intended for the individual's own enhancement. They are for the church, belong to the church, and have to be discerned by the church. The discernment in question is not simply that of the individual who is called to serve through this gift. It is the church which discerns who possesses these gifts and

this discernment devolves rather specifically upon a particular church or community. A person is not *delegated* by the church community to serve or to perform a mission. The person is first gifted by God for the mission, but the community has a responsibility, however, to discern the person's call and to express the community's readiness to incorporate this service into its life and mission. This is as true of the ordained as it is of the nonordained. To speak of a delegation would mean supporting either an oligarchical or a democratic system: since the church lives only by the power of Christ and of his Spirit, it is neither and its procedures cannot be modeled on the purely secular. For the church to fail, on the other hand, to use discernment would be to abrogate its corporate quality. It would leave way for a splintering of the reality which is the unity.

Discernment is allied with praxis. Such was the case in New Testament times. Only those gifts were acknowledged and received into the life of the body which were beneficial to it, and there was a hierarchy of gifts spelt out in terms of their value for the body. This is what Paul means in the latter section of his first letter to the Corinthians, and he had said substantially the same thing when writing of preachers, even while being ready to leave a certain amount to the Lord to judge on *His* day. The validity of ministry, to use the word loosely, is not assessed on the ground of its ecclesiastical provenance, but on the ground of its benefit to the church.

Today, with a resurgence of ministries and the development of the notion of mission, the procedure of discernment is more complex. It continues to judge how well a service meets the needs and promotes the mission of the church. The community must discern the gifts of its members in relation to its vision of the kingdom of God. What liberation theology says about the connection between mysticism and political commitment is pertinent to all Christian communities in the sense that the contemplation of the mystery of Christ and Christian action are inseparable. This, of course, does not entail for all communities the type of political option which is favored by liberation theology in Latin America, but these theologians do bring home to us the relation between adherence to the mystery and practical options.

The rightness of a practical option or a particular kind of service is not something that can be judged *a priori*, or legitimated *a priori*, on the simple basis that the power of decision lies only with institutional authority. When there is conflict between the charismatic and the institutional, the position of the authority cannot be immediately given preference on the plea that it is of divine origin or that it holds power from Christ. If order and baptism benefit from demysticization, the same can be said of juridical authority. Power does not indeed come from the people but from Christ, but the exercise of power which is given juridical form, like any other service in the church, needs to be subjected to periodic discernment, just as it needs to incorporate into its way of acting the principles of discernment.

At their meeting at Puebla, Mexico, in 1979, the Conference of Latin American Bishops (CELAM) expressed a fear that the laity's involvement in church matters might mean their withdrawal in large numbers from a vital concern for the secular arena. The conference also put restrictions on the involvement of religious, priests, and bishops in political affairs, for it seemed to the bishops that this could be the cause of scandal in the community or a factor leading to division. Theoretically, they appealed to the role of the clergy and religious to signify the unity of the community and its eschatological tension. This was the way in which the Puebla conference expressed the dilemma about the respective roles of laity and clergy, already present in the conciliar constitution on the church of Vatican II.

This dilemma can be resolved only by considering the action of the church community as a body, not by deciding what this, that or the other person ought to be or to do. Here again, it is helpful to remember that the renewal of ministries depends on the renewal of community as such. It is only where there is a vital sense of community that a question of this sort can be placed in its proper context. All are concerned about the same thing, presbyter and laity alike, and their action needs to appear as one, not divided. The role of the ordained minister is to represent *in the midst of this community* its work for the kingdom, its eschatological nature, and its relationship to Christ. Since its eschatological nature does not keep the church out of the world but expresses a mode of being in that world, the one who represents this quality need not be less concerned about the world than others. It may be wise for the ordained minister to avoid certain commitments, but it is not a theological principle that he must do so.

If ministry is viewed as the action of the eschatological fellowship for the kingdom in the midst of the world, there need be no fear that the laity will be torn between service in the church and action in the world in the name of the church. Indeed, today the person who is best suited to the liturgical ministry of reader (which includes the charism of teacher) might well be the one most involved in secular affairs. All has its basis in liturgy, and all has its finality in the transformation of the world. The secular not only need not destroy the eschatological and the mystical: it demands them. The mystical and the eschatological not only do not cause withdrawal from the world: they dictate participation, even while exacting a constant reassessment of such participation. The flowering of lay ministries does not have to result from a desire or an impulse to have more part in church life in an inward-looking way. It can, and often does, result from the impulse of the eschatological people, God's holy people, to have more part in the life of the world, for its salvation and for the glory of God.

In this chapter, I have sought to reflect upon the development of lay ministries as a grass-roots movement, postulating the restructuring of ministries. I have thus set a reflection on ministries in the context of the community in process of renewal. I have spoken of the need to reconsider our symbols of church membership and of service or ministry, so that it might be possible to understand all ministries, lay and ordained, on the basis of the symbol of the people, the holy and eschatological people of the covenant given in Jesus Christ and in his Spirit. The practical emergence of ministries will depend on how radical an experience of communion in Christ's word, in his hope and in his Spirit, is attained. No amount of structuring can replace the vital community in which service is rooted and the power of Christ experienced as grace.

By way of addendum, I would remark, as intimated in earlier chapters, that one of the reasons why the correlation of lay and ordained becomes confused is that many persons today exercise the role of presidency in community and liturgy without ordination. The limit placed on them is that of not being allowed a full eucharist. By one route or another, either by appointment by the clergy or by choice of the community, or by a mixture of both, they have acceded to a role which calls out for the laying-on of hands but remain unordained. The church's authority is unwilling as a rule to ordain anyone who is not male, celibate, seminary trained, and dependent on office for stipend and sustenance. We can go ahead for a long time with the status quo thus established by practice and accommodation, while pleading for more "vocations," when in fact the situation is telling us that the conception of the ordained minister is what needs to be changed.

1. On practices which only support the abiding ambiguity, see J.-L. Segundo, *The Hidden Motives of Pastoral Action*, translated from the Spanish (Orbis Books, New York 1978), 83-108.

2. S. Langer, *Philosophy in a New Key*, 3rd ed. (Harvard University Press, Cambridge, Mass. 1978).

3. Kavanagh, *The Shape of Baptism*, 109-110.

4. Kavanagh 22-23.

5. R. Otto, *The Idea of the Holy*, translated from the German by J. Harvey (Penguin Books, Middlesex, 1959), 98-99.

6. *Lumen gentium* 10: Flannery 361.

7. See especially, Augustine, *De Baptismo Libri Septem*, CSEL 51, 145-375.

8. See E. Schillebeeckx, *Christ the Sacrament of Encounter with God* (Sheed Andrews and McMeel, Kansas City 1963), 153-173. For Augustine's own use of the word "character" see N. Häring, "St. Augustine's Use of the Word 'Character,'" *Medieval Studies* 14 (1952) 79-97.

9. J.R. Villalón, *Sacrements dans l'Esprit: Existence Humaine et Théologie Existentielle* (Beauchesne, Paris 1977).

10. See Chapter Four, note 2.

11. *Presbyterorum ordinis* 2: Flannery 864.

12. See E. Kilmartin, "A Modern Approach to the Word of God and Sacraments of Christ: Perspectives and Principles," in F.A. Eigo, ed., *The Sacraments: God's Love and Mercy Actualized* (The Villanova University Press, Villanova 1979), 107: "The liturgical celebrant represents the church which is eschatologically sanctified. . . . The priest can act *in persona Christi* only by acting *in persona Ecclesiae*. He directly represents the church and so Christ who is the source of its being."

Chapter Six

Recognition of Ministries: Blessing and Commissioning

In treating the question of how lay ministers may be commissioned and blessed, it is helpful to recall some things which have become apparent in the course of the preceding chapters. Lay ministries flourish in the context of a community of faith endowed with a sense of mutual service and of mission. The question of lay ministries arises from such a milieu, rather than from a concern merely to increase the number of those willing to help presbyters and bishops in their tasks. Occasionally, it is in this latter way that the question is phrased, but this seems to miss the point. In short, in order to understand the reality of lay ministry we go first to the fact of community renewal, of which basic Christian communities are the most obvious but not the only instance. To take this as the proper context within which to treat of the theology of ministries and of their recognition is not to reduce ministry to a call from the community. In fact, service or ministry has an individual stamp because it bears the mark of the individual person and of the grace of the Spirit given to the person. The fact is that the gift of the Spirit is rooted in the baptism whereby a person becomes a member of the body of Christ, and as such is enabled to contribute to the life and mission of the community when the gift is virtually or formally recognized by the community.

One level at which a person's service or gift is recognized is that at which it is duly respected by the community at large and made use of in the activities of the community. Thereby arises the situation wherein "having gifts that differ according to the grace given to us, (we) use them: if prophecy, in proportion to our faith; if service, in our serving; he who teaches, in his teaching; he who exhorts, in his exhortation; he who contributes, in liberality; he who gives aid, with zeal; he who does acts of mercy, with cheerfulness" (Romans 12.6-8). Whoever can sing, sings; whoever can heal, heals; whoever can judge secular affairs with the eyes of faith and Christian discernment, discerns.

Often, this kind of recognition and assimilation is all that is necessary for mutual support and for sharing a mission. It is hard enough, of course, to realize in practice, since it supposes a great spirit of openness to one another's gifts and a readiness to support one another in mutual affirmation. It is often from others that a person comes to appreciate his or her own possession of the Spirit or of particular gifts. Experience shows that it is not the easiest thing to believe in one's own possession of the Spirit. Energy which is spent in stressing the need to discern and to control spirits might be usefully expended in persuading the faithful that they do indeed possess the Holy Spirit and his gifts.

The question which has been raised for the church, however, by the provisions of *Ministeria quaedam* concerns more formal modes of recognition. This is therefore the subject that will be treated in this chapter. A number of services actually exercised by lay persons bring up the matter of the discipline of ordination. This is particularly true of the leadership roles, involving both community and liturgical presidency, now filled by lay persons in various parts of the world. The present discipline of the church leaves many Christian communities in a situation wherein they have this kind of leadership but cannot have a full sacramental ministry. Many voices have been raised to say that the only adequate response to this living reality is to change the discipline. While agreeing with this proposal, I will not treat further of it, lest I wander from the subject of this work, which is lay ministry, that kind of service to the church which does not raise the subject of ordination.

What the churches have to ask themselves regarding the service of the laity is, whether some form of canonical and/or liturgical blessing is appropriate to some of the offices or charges assumed by lay persons. *Ministeria quaedam* and *Immensae caritatis* allow for two degrees of recognition and blessing, one for the offices of acolyte and reader, the other for special ministers of communion. In the first chapter, we saw that many other kinds of particular service have emerged in recent times, such as youth counseling, marriage counseling, teaching, interconfessional and interfaith dialogue, Christian action in the secular arena, and so on. Hence the question: what is the significance of the kind of recognition already given to the offices of acolyte and reader, and to the ministry of communion, and is it appropriate to give similar recognition to other offices and services?

By and large, there seem to be three possible kinds of church approval or mandate. *Ministeria quaedam* has constituted the offices of acolyte and reader as canonical offices to which persons are commissioned and for the exercise of which they are blessed through a formal liturgy. That is the first possibility. A second possibility is that of a commissioning and blessing without the concept of canonical office, as is the case for special ministers of the eucharist. A third possibility is that of a blessing which is the recognition of a charism and a charging of a person with a mission or service appropriate to the charism. This would occur, for example, if a person engaged in Christian action in the secular field were to be blessed by a community as a form of recognition and sending whereby the community acknowledges that person's action as its own. But in order to explore those possibilities in more depth, we should first of all take a look at the rites for the institution of acolyte and reader.

BLESSINGS AND INSTALLATIONS

The history of the blessing of candidates for lesser ministries or offices betrays some confusion as to their meaning for the church. The author of the *Apostolic Tradition* wished above all to distinguish between the threefold ministry of bishop, presbyter, and deacon on the one hand and minor offices on the other. Subdeacon, reader, and widow were not to receive a laying of hands. Following this lead, the main trend of East Syrian canonical literature is to see induction into lesser roles as a kind of commissioning to a function that is necessary or useful to the order of worship, but not constitutive of anything essential to it.

The *Apostolic Constitutions* is, however, something of an exception to this policy. The deaconess, the subdeacon, and the reader are to receive a laying-on of hands,[1] and installation into these offices has many other features of an ordination. In all three ceremonies, the presider prays for the gift of the Spirit to be given to the candidate. The three prayers of blessing invoke Old Testament paradigms for the ministry bestowed. In the case of the deaconess, these are holy women endowed with the gift of God's Spirit, namely, Miriam, Deborah, Hannah and Huldah, and the "guardians of the gates of the Temple." In the case of the subdeacon, the keepers of the ark of the covenant and the guardians of the sacred vessels serve as paradigm, and in the case of the reader it is Esdras's proclamation of the law to the people. As a further parallel with ordination, these three offices involve a liturgical service, intimated by the Old Testament paradigms. The deaconess has something to do with the keeping of the holy place, the subdeacon

148

with the keeping of the vessels used in worship, and the reader, of course, with the proclamation of the scriptures to the assembled people.

The compiler of the *Apostolic Constitutions* may inflate these functions somewhat by paralleling the installation into office with ordination. His reasoning appears to be that a service to the community, and especially to its worship, requires the gift of the Spirit, and since these offices imply such service they are to be in some way compared with the offices of bishop, presbyter, and deacon. However, the book remains an isolated witness to this form of blessing, and therefore also to the concept of office or ministry involved.

In the western church, the work that most influenced the history of the rites of installation was the *Statuta Ecclesiae Antiqua* of fifth-century Gaul.[2] Even while using the term *ordination* for induction into all offices, this work keeps the installation into the higher and lesser offices clearly distinct. Bishop, presybter, and deacon receive the laying-on of hands with the prayer of blessing. Others are commissioned without much ceremony. The bishop is to teach the acolyte what his office demands of him, and he is to receive from the archdeacon the instruments of his office. No words are given to accompany this action, although the description of the office given by the *Statuta* later became the form accompanying the giving of the instruments. The porter and exorcist are to be installed in a similar way. The reader is to be presented to the people by the bishop, and he receives his office when the bishop gives him the codex of the scriptures with an admonition to perform his task fittingly. The presentation of the reader to the people distinguishes this installation from the other three. This could reflect the fact that it was viewed somewhat differently to the others, since it involved a direct ministry to the people, unlike those of acolyte and porter. The role of the exorcist would not be exercised in the assembly and pertained only to those affected by evil spirits, and according to the prescriptions given he remained directly responsible to the bishop for whatever exorcisms he was to perform. Besides these four offices, the *Statuta* also mention the psalmist, who receives his office directly from the rural pastor rather than from the bishop, and the widows and holy women who are to help with the baptism of women, but these offices do not seem to require any formal installation ceremony.

The *Missale Francorum* of seventh- or eight-century Gaul has a double section concerning the installation of minor ministers. In the first section, it simply transcribes the text of the *Statuta Ecclesiae Antiqua* for porter, acolyte, and exorcist, leaving out any mention of the reader.[3] This section is juxtaposed with another, which provides blessings for porter, acolyte, reader, and exorcist, in that order, these being followed by a much more elaborate ordination of the subdeacon, making him a kind of midpoint between the lesser orders and the orders of deacon, presbyter, and bishop.[4]

The ceremony for the installation of the reader in this second section differs somewhat from the others, in that, whereas in the original *Statuta Ecclesiae Antiqua* the candidate is presented to the people, here he is said to be elected or chosen by the people. The blessing prayer, in all four cases, is quite unspectacular. It makes no mention of a gift of the Spirit to perform a ministry, but asks in a very straightforward way and without elaboration that God may bless the candidate in view of a rather specific description of the task to the performed, that is, to watch the doors of the church, to be an acolyte, to read the scriptures clearly and with devotion, and to impose hands on those inflicted by evil spirits. The only one of the prayers to include a biblical paradigm is that for the acolyte, which mentions the divine precept to Moses and Aaron to keep lamps lighting in the tabernacle.

The blessing for the subdeacon seems to reflect the way in which this office, almost identical in its origins with that of the acolyte, moves from the ranks of lesser offices to those of the hierarchical or sacred orders. Installation is by way of a giving of instruments, to wit an empty paten and chalice, but then there is a lengthy instruction, a *praefatio* and a blessing that resembles the blessings for the higher orders. True, there is no mention in it of the gift of the Holy Spirit, as in the cases of deacon, presbyter, and bishop, but the prayer does ask for the sevenfold gifts of wisdom, understanding, counsel, fortitude, knowledge, piety, and the fear of the Lord, which were associated with the gift of the Spirit. We do know, of course, that the increasing importance given to the order of subdeacon did not really come from anything intrinsic to the ministry but from the fact that the subdeaconate was the final state of preparation before the ascent to the order of deacon.

It was this Gallican material that was incorporated into the Roman rite's ordinal. The Gelasian Sacramentary keeps the citation of the *Statuta* separate from the prayers of blessing,[5] as does the *Missale Francorum*, but some copies of the eighth-century Gelasian models already make the words of the *Statuta* figure as a rubric that is joined with the blessing.[6] This became the established procedure in the tenth-century *Pontificale Romano-Germanicum* and in the later gallicanized pontificals of the Roman Curia.[7] The effect of this is to make the rite of installation the giving of instruments, together with the formula accompanying it, and to turn the blessing into an adjunct ceremony. It needs to be remarked, however, that in the major orders there was a contemporaneous transfer of attention from the blessing and the laying-on of hands to the giving of instruments and anointings. All the same, some difference remains. The anointings, vestings, and giving of insignia or instruments associated with the major orders come after the laying-on of hands and the blessing, whereas in the minor orders the giving of instruments precedes the blessing, which means that this kind of installation has a more obvious appearance of a commissioning to a function.

The blessing for the acolyte in the *Pontificale Romano-Germanicum* amplifies on the usage of biblical paradigm found in the *Missale Francorum*. It recalls the light that is given to the world through Christ and the apostles, as well as the blood and water that flowed from the side of Christ on the cross. These refer to the duties of the acolyte in lighting the candles and serving at the eucharistic table.

By and large, one would have to say that this early history of induction into lesser church offices reflects a form of commissioning to some specific function to be performed, rather than any ample notion of church ministry and accompanying gifts of grace. Despite the occasional presentation of a candidate to an assembly, or the use of a prayer of blessing, or an appeal to a biblical paradigm, the offices do not share in the understanding of ministry in and to the church associated with ordination. Induction into these offices is by assignation to a task, rather than by an invocation of the grace of the Spirit, and for the most part the tasks concern the performance of cult rather than the service of the people.

These rites of the *Pontificale Romano-Germanicum* were taken into the pontificals of the Roman Curia in later centuries, and remained virtually the same up to and including the Tridentine reform. They were thus in vogue until 1972, when Paul VI changed the discipline. The new rites issued that year by the Holy See explicitly state that the acolythate and lectorate are not to be considered as orders. The installation ceremony is entitled "institution" rather than ordination. Curiously enough, however, the revision has pursued the model of ordination even further than the Roman Pontifical of earlier centuries. Now, the commissioning or giving of instruments follows the blessing, instead of preceding it.[8] The parallel is thus perfect between ordination and the institution of these two offices: presentation of candidates, homily and exhortation, invitation to common prayer, blessing, supplementary rites.

Does this new disposition of the rite manifest an intention to give greater moment to blessing, thus placing less importance on the commissioning? Those who prepared the English translation of the texts obviously did not think so, since they have added a heading which does not belong in the original Latin text. Thus, though the entire rite is called *institution*, they have used the word *institution* again as a heading for the giving of the bible at the installation of a reader, and for the giving of the vessel with bread and wine at the installation of the acolyte.[9] This is to imply that these are the actions which constitute the essential part of the ceremony or the formal installation. The blessing is then implicitly interpreted as a prayer which implores God's grace on the candidate. It is not the act which confers the office, as in ordination.

One might justifiably argue that rites ought not to be split up into sections by such explanatory titles, but at the same time it must be agreed that the arrangement of the ICEL text seems correctly to reflect the intention of Paul VI and of those who compiled the ritual. For reasons which can well be left to each one to surmise, the Sacred Congregation for Divine Worship seems to have adopted the ordination model as a general model for public rites. It has found its way also into religious profession. Adopting the model, however, does not imply that it gives to the blessing of offices or to the blessing of religious the power and meaning which it gives to ordination prayers. Paul VI in his *motu proprio* gives the interpretation to be followed when he mentions that through these rites "functions [are] committed,"[10] or when he interprets liturgical history as follows: "The conferring of these functions often took place by a special rite, in which, after God's blessing had been implored, a Christian was established in a special class or rank for the fulfillment of some ecclesiastical function."[11] These texts say that it is not the blessing which constitutes a person in office, but the commissioning of functions and the establishment in a special class.

All of this leads to the conclusion that the installations of acolyte and reader are seen in present church practice as a commissioning to special functions by the bishop. The special ministers of the eucharist are spoken of in the same way in *Immensae caritatis*. At the same time, these ministries have been presented as a way of following up on the Vatican Council's intention to involve the laity more in the ministry of the church, and most particularly in liturgical ministry. If such ministry is a way of exercising the call received in baptism, what can justify this commissioning? Why is it necessary to commission lay persons, and even to set up special canonical offices, for services which are normally theirs in virtue of their membership of the Christian community? Some discipline and control may be necessary, but hardly a canonical office or a commissioning and appointment in such official form. There are only two broad genders of liturgical ministry: that which is attached to baptism and that which is attached to order. To serve at the table, to give communion to others, to bring the communion to the sick, to read the scriptures, to instruct in doctrine, to make the word known to non-Christians, are not tasks which require a commissioning over and above baptism and the gifts of the Spirit. Their exercise has indeed to be regulated by proper community discipline, but this is a different thing from a canonical or semi-canonical

154

commissioning. Not much attention has in fact been given to the offices of acolyte and reader. Their existence appears to be superfluous once there grows the understanding of what it means to be Christian and a member of the body of the Lord. The earliest case of the appointment of a reader seems to have been a matter of discipline and control, but later in the middle ages the reader and his colleagues became men who shared in a lesser way in what was perceived as the office of major orders. The process was no doubt made easier by reason of the fact that the major orders also took on something of the appearance of a commissioning to specific functions. In any case, this understanding provided the justification for the existence of minor orders and for a ceremony of installation. It sits rather uneasily today with those who have come to look upon the role of reader and acolyte as lay functions. A lay office does not need this jurisdiction, no more than jurisdiction ought to be used to supply for order, as happens when lay people are commissioned to preside at Sunday services, officiate at weddings, and the like.

THE PRACTICE OF OTHER CHURCHES

In recent years other Christian confessions in the United States have developed a ritual of blessings for ministries in the church, with which it is possible to compare the Roman Catholic ritual.

In 1984, the United Methodist Church, following up on previous work, published a book of *Blessings and Consecrations* to be included among its supplemental worship resources.[12] Among the blessings that concern ministry are an order for commitment to Christian service, an order for the certification of associates, directors or ministers of education and associates, directors or ministers of music, an order for the recognition of leaders in the church, an order for the recognition of church social workers, and finally an order for the recognition of those engaged in music ministries.

155

The introduction to this booklet offers a brief theology of blessing and consecration that serves to explain the format of these services. There are three major elements to this theology. First of all, the text affirms and upholds the fundamental consecration of baptism, by which the Christian becomes a member of the royal priesthood and from which flow gifts of the Spirit and of service. Secondly, it teaches that there are a variety of ways in which this one consecration is realized in the life of the church, so that there is room for special dedications and consecrations, which are rooted in baptismal consecration. Thirdly, it proposes the eucharistic blessing of the bread and wine as the paradigm for all blessings. Hence it gives this description of blessings and consecrations, which applies to blessings of ministers as to all others contained in the book:

"The purpose of *Blessings and Consecrations* is to recognize some of the varieties in which the one consecration in Christ is realized in the life of the church. The services provided in this collection are not exhaustive of the possibilities for liturgical acts of dedication and consecration. Other liturgies, composed by groups or individuals for special purposes, are possible and desirable. Such services, or 'moments' within services, help the Christian community recognize its identity and mission."[13]

In the ritual order provided for these services, the main core is the commitment to task asked of the candidate. The acceptance or reception by the congregation is integral to the order. In no case, does the collection offer a specific text for a blessing prayer, even when it mentions that such should be made. As already mentioned, however, the introduction sees the eucharistic blessing as the paradigm, so that presumably other blessings would adopt the format where "thanks are given for all that God has done, is

156

doing, and will do in Jesus Christ,"[14] and God's grace is invoked upon the blessing's recipients. However, the theology of blessing given in the introduction is cautious about the efficaciousness of blessing, when it remarks that "no ceremony properly executed in and of itself alone becomes the guarantor . . . of the actuality of consecration and dedication."[15] The blessing is seen mostly as a recognition of divine presence and a celebration of it, or indeed as an experience of the power of which it speaks.

The desire to avoid attributing any magical efficacy to blessings is here evident, as is also a reluctance to use language that may sound akin to the Catholic notion of *ex opere operato* efficacy. The idea that a blessing is first of all a recognition of divine presence and action in the church or world, or more specifically in the life of a person blessed, is fundamental to ecclesial tradition. However, this particular Methodist theology of consecration may evacuate blessing of any power of change rather too drastically. While ritual and prayer are properly rooted in a discernment of the Spirit's action and in the church's experience of it, they do have some transformative effect. The mere fact that the experience is brought to expression within a specific setting of ecclesial gathering and remembrance cannot leave the experience and the person blessed unchanged. The Spirit acts in the church through the communion of persons, and through the words and actions that shape that communion and its Christian meaning.

In the *Occasional Services*, which the Inter-Lutheran Church Commission in the United States published in 1982 as a complement to the *Lutheran Book of Worship*, some distinctions between ministries determine the format of blessings for persons engaged in church service.[16] Some rituals are for the commissioning of lay professionals, who take on a full-time engagement or what is called a major occupational commitment within the church. Others envisage the recognition of ministries that do not involve this major occupational commitment, even though the type of work is similar, as for example, a ministry of teaching. A third type of service is for the installation of elected parish officers, and there is still a fourth kind of liturgy that is an affirmation of the vocation of Christians in the world. This can be used on almost any occasion when people wish to affirm the Christian stance of their life commitment, whether it be in the family, in the service of government, in commerce, in farming, in industry, in the arts, and so forth.

One notices the difference between the terms by which these services are designated, namely, commissioning, recognition, installation, and affirmation. These terms apparently imply a diversified sense of how the ministries involved belong in the life of the church. A commissioning is given to those whose identity is shaped by their service of the church because this is a full-time engagement, although the fields in which this is undertaken are as divergent as medical work, Christian education, youth ministry, music ministry, and administration. The work that the person undertakes is the work that the church as a body has undertaken. In the recognition of ministries, the church congregation recognizes those in its midst who serve its life in worship, in learning, in services of different sorts, in witness, and in stewardship, even though this does not involve a major occupational commitment. It sees this ministry inspired by the Spirit, done in the Spirit, and requiring the constant grace of the Spirit. An installation involves election of such persons as church council members, and hence involves not only congregational approval but also a representational role in the government of the church. Lastly, the service of affirmation of the vocation of Christians in the world is rooted in a theology of witness, and in the recognition that the presence of Christ is active in all human affairs through the dedication and witness of believers.

The format of the service in each case has the commitment requested of, and given by, the person blessed as its core. The euchology of the services emphasizes invocation of God's grace over thanksgiving, which is relatively infrequent and secondary. The invocations, however, start by recognizing the workings of God's grace, the divine order of the church established in Christ, and the special gifts that the Spirit distributes among the faithful. In this sense, a recognition of divine deeds in history and in the present, and of God's grace in the lives of the baptized who assume ministry, or give witness, is the basis of the blessings.

A fairly typical prayer for the commissioning of lay professionals is the following, destined for the blessing of directors of Christian education and of youth ministers:

"Almighty and ever-living God, as you called apostles and evangelists, pastors and teachers to instruct, comfort, admonish and care for us, so you have called this your servant. Fill him/her with wisdom and patience, with love and faithfulness to your Word, that he/she may with gladness teach, comfort, counsel, and guide your people to full maturity in Christ Jesus, Your Son, our Lord."[17]

On the other hand, in the service for the recognition of ministries in a congregation, all invocations are to conclude with this brief thanks and prayer:

"For all who offer themselves in your name, we give thanks, O God. Give them the joy of service, and constant care and guidance. Help us all to be both willing servants and thankful recipients of ministry, that your name be glorified, your people live in peace, and your will be done; through Jesus Christ our Lord."[18]

What is the general sense of this collection of blessings, envisaging quite a variety of different ministerial commitments? It is obvious enough that all ministry and Christian witness is rooted in baptism and membership of the congregation of faith. Hence, while a major involvement in works that the church undertakes as a corporate body is given special recognition, there is no suggestion that other believers are any less called to the service of God, or act less as Christian people. Whether it be the explicit service of church word, worship, or *diakonia*, or whether it be a Christian presence of witness and care in the work of government or of the arts, everyone partakes in the life of Christ and in the work of the church for humanity's evangelization. Blessings and commitments at the appropriate stages of one's life, or as expressions of a community's identity and awareness of the Spirit, are ways of spelling out the meaning of the Christian calling and of asking God's continued grace and gift upon those called, in whatever form of service they have undertaken or are about to undertake. If the promise of dedication and commitment figures so prominently in the services, this would appear to be in keeping with the traditional Lutheran sense that all Christian life is a living out of baptism and a personal confirmation of the call and divine promise given thereby.

SOME ROMAN CATHOLIC OBSERVATIONS
The Lutheran and Methodist churches can, of course, root their present practice in the priority given by the Reformation to the priesthood of all the baptized, and in the sole designation of baptism and the Lord's supper as sacraments. While both traditions recognize

160

the historical character and importance of the ordained ministry of word and sacrament, they do not
take this to be a sacrament, but find that it is itself
founded in baptismal priesthood and in a special divine call to service. Because of their particular tradition and belief, Roman Catholics are more anxious to
keep the difference between ordained ministry and
other ministries, and hence between ordination services and other blessings for ministry and witness.
Through its own recent experience of ministries,
however, and through its likewise recent development of theological consciousness, there are two
things that the Roman Catholic community now
shares with Reformation traditions. The first of these
is the idea that ordained ministry needs to be related
to the baptismal call and to the grace of the Spirit that
calls forth and separates, so that ordination is not divorced from this double grounding. The second is the
consciousness of the diversity of ministries that exist
in the church alongside that of the ordained, and
whose presence and importance emerge through the
growing practice of liturgical commitment and blessing. While the official books of the Roman liturgy
contain only blessings for acolytes, readers, and ministers of communion, local dioceses and individual
communities are developing a variety of liturgies that
are not unlike those found in the worship resources
of the Lutheran and Methodist churches.

Some comparison between these blessings and ordination is inescapable. In the sacrament of order as
well as in the blessing of lay ministers, there has to
be a recognition of the prior gifts and call of the
Spirit. Indeed, it is a cornerstone of a current renewal
of ordained ministry and selection for ministry that
more attention needs to be given to the possession of
these gifts on the part of those aspiring to ordination.
The prayer of blessing in ordination, whatever its
particular format, is to begin with a recognition of the

workings of the Spirit in the church and in the life of the candidate, as these are discerned in the remembrance of Jesus Christ and God's deeds in him. The invocation of the enduring power of the Spirit in the work and life of the minister is rooted in the cognizance of the gifts that the person possesses and has already exercised within the community of the faithful, who can therefore recognize in the candidate a chosen one of God.

In all of this there is a similarity between ordination and the blessing of other ministers. The distinction between one and the other lies in the precise nature of the ministry to which the candidate is called and which is formally recognized, before God and with the invocation of God's Spirit, in liturgy. It is the representative nature of the ordained ministry, with its special relation to eucharistic ministry, that differentiates it from other ministries. In the celebration of the eucharist, and in other liturgical and sacramental acts related to this central Christian service, the ordained minister acts as representative of the believing community and thus as representative of Christ's action, power, and presence in it. The bishop and the presbyter have other ministries of teaching, leading, and directing, but it is their place in the liturgical assembly, whereby they signify its oneness in Christ and its apostolic and catholic character that is maintained only in the grace of the Spirit, that makes their ministry distinctive and in the proper sense of the word sacramental. It is then this liturgical role that qualifies and gives special moment to the other deeds of ministry that they enact in their daily service of the church. Although the theology of the deaconate has been much less clearly worked out, it seems correct to say in the light of tradition that the deacon represents, through his particular liturgical service in providing the bread and the wine, the full integration into the oneness of Christ's body of all the church's deeds of service and charity and stewardship. The provision of the bread and the wine for the celebration of the Lord's Supper has meaning and reality within the context of the provision of all human needs in the womb of a community of mutual service and charity. The deacon's supervision of such service in daily life goes with the eucharistic ministry that he performs in the assembly, and it is this latter service that shows the meaning of the former.

Once this distinction or difference between the significance of the ordained ministry and of other ministries is recognized, there does seem to be room in current ecclesial practice for a widespread and diversified use of blessings for ministers. The Lutheran and Methodist services set the proper tone inasmuch as they relate all witness and ministry, as well as all spiritual gifts, back to the fundamental consecration of baptism and to membership in God's covenant people, but at the same time show a recognition of the diversity of calls in that one people and the particularity of each individual's service. In recognizing the gifts of its individual members, the church celebrates its communion in the one Spirit of Christ. The community is the dwelling place of God's Spirit, the living sign in the midst of the world of the outpouring of the Spirit on all flesh and the beginnings of a new creation. It is within the community, in its prayer of assembly, that the presence of the Spirit is known and made manifest and that all the members are enriched by the communion thus celebrated. Because the liturgy is the church's recognition and affirmation of the Christian call, as it takes particular shape and form in the life of its members, we can certainly speak of the community empowering its members through the blessing given in God's name. This is not in any way contrary to the fact that the giving of the blessing is inspired by the recognition of the already-present action of the Spirit in the charismatic service and gifts of the person or persons blessed. Their recognition and integration into the liturgy in which the whole life of the church is celebrated and represented is itself a further empowerment. empowerment.

As far as the new liturgical books of the Roman Catholic church are concerned, then, taking note of the intention behind the blessings for acolytes, readers, and ministers of communion, one can see them as opening up possibilities for the blessing of ministers on a larger scale. Since there is no particular reason why a blessing should be reserved to these particular ministries, the habit of blessing other persons as well can be commended. In face of the flowering of new kinds of ministry in churches and confessions, we need ways to acknowledge that we are living in a new age of the Spirit. A general feeling of praise and thanksgiving is alive in many communities and this finds expression in liturgies of blessing. Sometimes, the desire for order creeps into these services and they are given the form of an ecclesiastical commissioning, with the subtle suggestion that a minister needs this power to take on the ministry. That seems to be particularly the case with a designation to liturgical ministries and with the assumption of major and full-time occupational commitments, as though in such instances a person were taking on something proper to ordained ministry. This is a questionable assumption, however, and for this reason services that indicate blessing and personal commitment seem preferable to those that suggest official commissioning by church authorities. It may be the place of authority to recognize and affirm the undertaking of tasks in the church, but hardly to commission.

On another plane, the Methodist service book suggests a good approach when it refrains from giving specific texts for blessing prayers but simply commends the practice, pointing to the eucharist as the model for church prayer. Perhaps it could have usefully given some texts that work out the model further for the blessing of persons engaging in ministry, simply because the knowledge of ecclesial prayer traditions in many communities is not great. It is this after all that forms the basis of good euchology and ritual: a knowledge of the prayer tradition, and good discernment of spirits that is sensitive in the particularities of the Spirit's inspiration in our time, and a wise leadership that moderates and directs the practice of communities.

THE FORMAT OF BLESSINGS

A word about the ecclesial tradition of blessing persons is here appropriate, difficult as it is to do so briefly. Studies on the eucharistic prayer in early local and cultural traditions have served as a good reminder that this prayer is the exemplar of all church blessing. At the same time, as these studies progress it is becoming increasingly apparent that there is considerable diversity in eucharistic prayer from one church tradition to another in early Christian times. At one stage, it was common to evoke the *berakah* as the model of the eucharistic prayer and this was taken to be a prayer of praise rendered to God for past and present graces. Subsequently, argument arose as to whether the *berakah* was a prayer of praise or a prayer of thanksgiving, and as to how far and in what way the Jewish table prayers serve as a prototype for Christian eucharist. More recently, some authors make appeal not to table prayers but to the *todah* of psalm or temple worship, in which the great deeds of God in the history of the people are recalled and acclaimed and God's benign remembrance of the people is invoked. As the study of eucharist takes in more traditions, attention has also been drawn to prayers whose format is primarily that of epiclesis or invocation of the blessing of the Spirit on the gifts. This, of course, means that in looking to the eucharistic anaphora as the model for all blessing, we have to be aware that we are not dealing with a uniform tradition or with a stereotype. This makes the development of prayers within an established church tradition both more difficult and much richer.

From the variety of studies on the anaphora, in as much as this is pertinent to the present issues, several guidelines can be drawn. First of all, the prayer is made in remembrance of God's salvific deeds, and, in Christian times, in the persuasion of the eschatological blessing that is given to the world in Jesus Christ, the assurance of God's saving love and the promise of the fulfillment of divine promise. In the second place, the prayer invokes the power of that Spirit whose action in our midst is guaranteed by the mysteries of Christ that are remembered. In the third place, the prayer is the celebration of the mystery of the church, as God's people, the body of Christ, the communion in God's Spirit. In the fourth place, while the liturgy evokes and celebrates the redemptive mystery in its fullness, it belongs to a particular community and expresses the action of divine grace in the persons and things and events of a particular time and place. Beyond these points, it still seems open to question as to whether the prayer should give the dominant place to praise, to thanksgiving, or to the invocation of the Spirit, and indeed as to whether or not all three types of expression ought to have a place in every prayer. The most fundamental thing is that the assurance of present grace is rooted in the remembrance of the Christ event and its eschatological promise of divine fulfillment.

In actual fact, when we look at the ordination prayers known to us from different traditions, we see that the dominant format is that of the invocation of the Spirit upon the candidate. However, the earlier the prayer the more clearly this invocation is grounded in the remembrance of the divine deeds that are taken to mark

166

the beginnings or types of church ministry. Thus in the *Apostolic Tradition*, the ordination prayer for a bishop[19] recalls the choosing of princes, priests, and levites in the Old Testament dispensation, and the sending of the Spirit upon the apostles and the powers to forgive sins, to bind and loose, and to choose ministers, given to them. In a particular way, it evokes the image of the high priest called to offer sacrifice. These types constitute an amalgam of the blessings that seem appropriate to the office of bishop. It is the remembrance of God's guidance of the Old Testament people by chosen persons, and of the outpouring of the Spirit of Christ upon the apostles, that motivates the assurance of present grace and the invocation of the Spirit upon the candidate for the episcopacy. At the same time, the reader of this text is conscious of the fact that a description of office is taking form and that the biblical remembrance serves the underpinning of this office. That by the time of the *Apostolic Tradition* a sense of the charismatic element in the church was on the wane is further expressed in the approach to lesser offices, where persons are designated to clearly defined ecclesiastical tasks, without the laying-on of hands.

The Roman liturgy of ordination in the texts of the Verona Sacramentary[20] shows more of a consciousness of forms and models for office than of a history developing constantly in the power of the Spirit. The ordination prayers are not couched in the form of thanksgiving, but in that of an amplified invocation. That is to say, after an opening address to God there follows a lengthy clause beginning with the word *qui* (who), into which the remembrance of past graces and deeds is incorporated. The prayers recall the ordinances for ministers of the temple in the Old Testament and the division of priests and levites, as well as the seventy elders appointed to help Moses, and from New Testament times the apostles and their helpers. Rather than being taken as stories that express the assurance that God will continue to come to the people's aid and service as needed, these all seem to serve as models that identify and conceptualize church office and its divisions. Already from such an early stage of history, the church is asking the gift of the Spirit for the candidate of an office whose nature it tries to clearly define, and expresses little expectation of the development of new forms of ministry.

Therefore, although the memorial of God's action in history, the recall of biblical images and stories, and the invocation of the Spirit that are found in ordination prayers give some indication of what the format of new blessings for newly discerned ministries might be, the model is limited by the fact that it does not allow for the new and unexpected, or for the eschatological hope of a future that is constantly unfolding before those who remember the newness of God's revelation in Jesus Christ, and the freshness of the power of the Spirit.

For this reason, some are turning to biblical blessings to look for a better paradigm than that provided in liturgical history. The examples are many and generally have to do with specific incidents or events. Noah blesses his sons (Gn 9.26–27); Balaam blesses Israel (Nm 23.8,20); Jacob blesses the sons of Joseph (Gn 48.15f.); Moses blesses the tribes of Israel (Dt 33.1ff.); Deborah blesses Jael, who saved Israel from its enemies in the killing of Sisera (Jgs 5.1ff.); David blesses his own house (2 Sm 6.20), and Huldah blesses the king of Judah (2 Kgs 22.11-20). Of these blessings, it can be noted that they occur within the context of covenant and mark God's dealings with the covenant community. Moreover, they are connected with a particular event, in which the one who blesses reads the signs of God's mercy and providence, and the assurance of a future for those who live in the hope of the divine promise. The identity of the person blessed within the covenant people is connected with the event recalled and is expressed in the blessing. Jacob spells out the fortunes of Joseph's sons, which is theirs because of the role that their father played in the fortunes of the people. Jael is to be remembered for all time through the deed in which she took God's part in acting for the people. The identity of the person and the identity of the people are reciprocal to one another.

The interlacing of covenant remembrance, awareness of a divine presence in an event, the identity of the people being shaped through this and other events, and the new identity given to those who act in God's power for and among the people, are the things that might well be brought to the fore in the blessing of new ministers for new ministries. Models of the past in which the congregation of the faithful was depicted as inferior to the one chosen are giving way to models for the future, wherein the person finds an identity and a call through the discernment of the community and through a faithful commitment to the furthering of its mission and witness. Models of the past in which office and its tasks are clearly depicted are giving way to models for the future in which the church is guided by eschatological hope and the belief that it will not be left deprived of the gifts and ministries that an as yet unknown future will require from it. Out of ancient roots a fresh liturgical practice is being fashioned.

Is it appropriate to practice a laying-on of hands for the blessing of nonordained ministers? This question is pertinent for the simple reason that some communities do lay hands on practically all candidates for ministry, of whatever type. In apostolic times, it would seem, the laying-on of hands did constitute a recognition of gift, an incorporation of this gift into the community's life in the Spirit, and a sending to act in the community's name. Apart from occasions of

ministerial recognition, it was a gesture used widely
to signify and invoke God's action and the blessings
of the Spirit on the new community and on its members, whether in sickness, in the forgiveness of sin,
or in the passing on of God's blessings from one generation to the next. It was later that in the context of
ministry the laying-on of hands was taken to be distinctive of the apostolic ministry and the higher orders. Provided the particular meaning of the apostolic
ministry is in some way expressed and retained,
there is no compelling reason to forbid a laying-on of
hands in the recognition and furthering of other ministries, in a way that parallels its use in baptism, confirmation, the blessing of the sick, the blessing of
children by parents, and the like.

CONCLUSION
By looking at the past history of blessings for office
and by considering some present trends, in Catholicism and in other churches, this chapter has offered
some reflections on the liturgical blessing of those
chosen in the Spirit to give witness and to minister
among God's people. The practice is still taking shape
because churches are only gradually learning to formulate in prayer and worship a newfound sense of
how the power of the Spirit ever constitutes anew the
life and identity of the eschatological people of God's
reign.

NOTES
1. *Apostolic Constitutions,* Book VIII, 19–22, Funk, ed., vol.
1, pp. 524–527.

2. *Statuta Ecclesiae Antiqua,* Munier, ed., canons 94–96, pp.
96–98.

3. L. C. Mohlberg, *Missale Francorum* (Herder, Rome 1957)
3–5.

4. *Missale Francorum* 6.

5. L. C. Mohlberg, *Liber Sacramentorum Romanae Aeclesiae Ordinis Anni Circuli* 737–756.

6. Cf. Andrieu, *Ordines Romani* III, p. 596.

7. C. Vogel and R. Elze, *Le Pontifical Romano-Germanique du Dixième Siècle* (Vatican City 1963), vol. I, pp. 12–19.

8. *The Rites* 740–745.

9. *The Rites* 742, 745.

10. *The Rites* 729.

11. *The Rites* 726.

12. *Blessings and Consecrations. A Book of Occasional Services,* Supplemental Worship Resources 14 (Abingdon, Nashville 1984).

13. *Blessings and Consecrations* 13.

14. *Blessings and Consecrations* 14.

15. *Blessings and Consecrations* 13.

16. *Occasional Services,* prepared by the churches participating in the Inter-Lutheran Commission on Worship (Augsburg, Minneapolis 1982).

17. *Occasional Services* I–45.

18. *Occasional Services* II–62.

19. *Apostolic Tradition,* Botte, ed. pp. 4–11.

20. For a study of these prayers, cf. David N. Power, *Ministers of Christ and His Church* (Chapman, London 1969).

Chapter Seven

Liturgical Ministries

Not long after Paul VI had issued his *motu proprio* on lay ministries in the liturgy, an Italian daily newspaper printed a photograph of a nun distributing holy communion. The caption explained that it was possible for her to do this, first of all because she had received the necessary power from the Pope, and secondly because being unmarried it was all right for her to touch the sacred host. Amusing though the incident may sound, it brings out the tendency to think of ministry in stereotypes. Pope Paul wanted to crack the stereotypes, but we have seen that the rites which he promulgated do not entirely avoid the notion that the laity need delegation in order to exercise liturgical ministries. He did, however, call for more thought and exploration which would further develop the practical consequences of the principles enunciated by the Second Vatican Council on lay participation and ministry in the liturgy. By retaining from what used to be called the minor orders the two ministries of acolyte and reader, he called the church's attention to two important types of lay liturgical action. It seems to me that we can go beyond the norms for these specific offices by considering what they point to in a more general way, namely, eucharistic hospitality and service of the word.

VIGILANCE AND HOSPITALITY
A good setting in which to consider lay liturgical service is that offered by 1 Peter 4.7-11. Some exegetes believe that this part of the letter is a series of admonitions relative to the nature and conduct of gatherings for wor-

ship.[1] As might be expected, the writer exhorts his
readers (or his hearers, if this be a homily) to the practice
of love, and draws a picture of the Christian gathering
as a community of love. Within that gathering, two matters are of particular interest to him. The first is that the
believers be vigilant in prayer, the second that they
practice mutual hospitality and care, since these are
necessary to the building up of a good household.

The first exhortation is to vigilance. This attitude of
mind has to be understood in relation to the New Testament parables on stewardship, vigilance, and the coming kingdom. When used of prayer and prayer gatherings, the word does not simply count as a synonym for
perseverance or assiduity. The alternate translation of
the original Greek, "sobriety," is helpful. To be sober is
to be watchful, that is, in full possession of one's senses,
on the ready, quick to note what is going on, or alert to
what is just around the corner. The writer's admonition
to vigilance can be related to the term "vigil" in its liturgical meaning. This suggests and inculcates an attitude
of awaiting, readiness, expectation. The great vigils of
the liturgical cycle, or vigils of prayer accompanied by
fast, or the vigils which wake the dead, are in line with
the thought of the letter.

The preacher who wished to admonish an audience to
vigilance in those early Christian times may have had a
comparatively easy task. The startling news of the kingdom fulfilled in Jesus Christ was fresh, the expectation
of the end not yet diminished. Our own times might
respond more heartily to the wailings of Daniel, when
he bemoaned the loss of prophet and priest to Israel
(Daniel 3.3 ff.). The people were then left without the
cult which celebrated their liberation, and without a
prophet to interpret the Lord's doings, to tell their story,
to recount their hopes. We might similarly ask what
poet, what prophet, what priest, can reveal the intima-
tions of immortality in so mortal a day as ours.

There are not wanting those who think that a revival of Verdi's *Requiem* or Handel's *Messiah* or of Gregorian chant are necessary to this task. While continuing to enjoy such works of art, however, we might find it profitable to harken to the second admonition of this pericope: Be hospitable. This is of the essence for a gathering of worshipers. It could be paraphrased in many ways: create a place for one another, make even the stranger welcome, share yourselves and what you have. Vigilance does not distract us from one another, but enhances mutual attentiveness. One of the primary images of worship in the New Testament is that of messianic table-fellowship. That certainly suggests mutual care and concern, as it simultaneously speaks of vigilance. In one of its renderings, the persons around the table have their loins girt, ready to set out on pilgrimage from the place where they eat. In another rendering, the room is on the threshold of the garden of Gethsemane. The meat and drink on the table are always important, since they address the company not only on the subject of fellowship but also on that of relation to the land which they are about to leave and to that for which they hope. There is a tension between being at home because of reciprocal hospitality, and taking the meeting place as temporary dwelling, a tent on the edge of a garden where mysteries lurk and into which one may step without ever returning.

Prophet, poet and hospitaler are names which might aptly describe those who serve in the assembly for worship. They are not the names of office, but are descriptive of qualities and attitudes. They largely represent the cares envisaged in setting up such offices as those of reader, psalmist, acolyte, doorkeeper—or today, such as those of usher and music director.

WORD AND WORSHIP
The primacy of word in worship, and the plurality of forms which it demands, cannot be too heavily em-

phasized. This is not for verbosity's sake, but in order that the power of the word, and its essential conjunction with creative imagination, may be grasped. Memorial is kept, the Spirit breathes, the Lord's death is proclaimed. Certainly, there are traditional elements to be observed, specific words to be spoken, definite things to be used, age-old rituals to be enacted. On a whole, however, Christian worship is relatively uncluttered by niggling traditions. It is the prayer of free persons, a worship in the Spirit who gives freedom in love and mystery. The external word depends on the inner word, that which is sealed in the anointing of the Spirit and which is spoken from the heart.

While the scriptures stand at the heart of liturgy, as a word heard, listened to, received, it is in virtue of the inner word that memory is kept alive, kerygma proclaimed, prophecy spoken, thanksgiving rendered. The Christian religion is no cyclic religion, conforming humanity to the patterns of the seasons and the influence of cosmic bodies. It is dominated instead by a sense of the Lord's *kairos*, of his imminence in all things and in all moments. It is a utopia which finds that tongues are newly loosened in God's praise, and that simple things, like bread and wine, water and oil, talk to us most eloquently of our relation in Christ to earth, sky and mortality.

The role of priest and president apart, the ministry of all members of the community to the word is that of drawing on the creative inner word of faith and on the skills and gifts which are peculiar to each one. Creativity is certainly highlighted in the task of the one who presides, teaches, interprets and gives thanks, but there are many other word ministries which converge with his to express the presence of Christ and his Spirit in the act of worship. Paul described worship as a singing of psalms and canticles in praise and thanksgiving, and in 1 Corinthians he had much to say about the various gifts of the Spirit which are used in the assembly in mutual service. Were we today to make a list of services to one another in the word of God, we would have to include Paul's list and others besides. Some mention would need to be made of music in all its forms, of dance and the use of plastic arts. All of these have to do with the proclaiming of the Lord's love, keeping the memory of Christ, interpreting or expressing the people's history and the nature of their earthly dwelling.

It is the sense of history which is given expression in liturgy that makes it so vital to the discernment spoken of in earlier chapters. The discernment is multiple. It has to do with the community's stance on temporal and political questions, as it has to do with the recognition of the gifts which the Spirit bestows on its members. In the final analysis, it is only as worshiping community that the Christian body discerns its place in the secular arena and its part in human history as sacrament of the kingdom of God. This is why the distinction between the priest's devotion to divine service and the lay person's dedication to the temporal has to be constantly mitigated. This is not, of course, to state that specific decisions are to be made in the course of worship, nor that no political pluralism is possible among members of the same gathering. This would be manifestly false. The point at issue is rather that it is within a common horizon, in the sharing of the common concerns brought to surface through the word heard, proclaimed and celebrated, that Christians serve the world.

One of the issues currently raised is whether lay persons may preach, or be fittingly delegated to preach, in the liturgical assembly. The issue has received most attention in the dispositions taken by the German episcopate, as earlier noted, and in their correspondence with the Holy See on the subject. As is remarked in this documentation, there are already many ways in which the laity share in the communication of the word in the assembly. They may give some explanation of the scriptures, they may give personal testimony, they may formulate prayers pertinent to the day's texts. All of this has become a normal and common way for the laity to give expression to their belief and their hearing of God's word, given the right kind of community and environment. It is also part of the description of the official reader's office that he instruct others in the knowledge of the scriptures, part of which could be presumably done in the assembly.

The particular matter of concern for the German bishops, however, as well as in other pertinent literature, is whether or not a lay person can give the homily at a liturgical celebration. What is here understood is the comment on the scriptures that is given immediately after the proclamation of the Gospel, and that is liturgically integral to this proclamation. Historically, this has always been part of the presider's role. There was a time when only the bishop gave the homily. Even presbyters replacing him in presiding at the eucharist were not allowed to do so, since to assume the bishop's role as head and teacher of the church in so full a way would be equivalent to a challenge to the unity of the church.

The ecclesiological and liturgical attitudes behind such dispositions are clear. The unity of the assembly is signified in its presidency, and the unity of word and sacrament in liturgical celebration is likewise maintained in the person and action of the presider. At a time when there were ample opportunities for all the faithful to exercise their charisms of service, including those of word, in favor of the community, both within and outside the liturgy, this liturgical pattern of reserving the homily as well as the blessing prayer to the presider would not have been experienced as a stifling of gifts.

In today's liturgical practice, comment and interpretation of the word is usually restricted to the homily, with the effective absence of any voice other than that of the presider. Hence, the issue of the preaching of the laity within the liturgy is raised from two different points of view. First of all, it is looked at from a practical point of view, as in the case of the German bishops. The practical arguments for allowing some part to the laity in giving homilies have to do with the decreasing number of priests and the high level of religious culture among large numbers of the baptized. Even the new Code of Canon Law provides for a liturgical presidency and an exercise of the ministry of the word by lay persons in the absence of the ordained.[2] The theological argument behind this approach is similar to what was proposed in the preconciliar theology of Yves Congar. It is argued that it is part of the laity's baptismal call that they can be fittingly delegated to this particular kind of immediate cooperation in the functions of the bishop and the priest.

From a second point of view, however, this argumentation is specious, for it fails to address the real issue, which is that of the demand put upon the church to allow the gifts of the Spirit given to the baptized to be exercised properly. The ordering of the assembly cannot be determined by the principles of law alone. The discernment and exercise of spiritual gifts have their part to play as well. Today, it is evident that many of the baptized are gifted and called to present and interpret the meaning of God's word, as proclaimed in the scriptures and active in the lives of the faithful.[3] Room must be made, therefore, to allow lay persons to give the homily at the eucharist and at other liturgical services.

The question needs to be seen in relation to a proper understanding of liturgical structure. There is no necessary conflict between the ordained minister's presidency of liturgy that comprises work and sacrament as necessary complements to one another, and the participation of the laity in sacramental and word

178

ministries. The call of the laity to minister, as it is taking shape within our time, needs to be properly integrated into a liturgy in which the presider's role is also taking on a new shape. In practice, in places where the laity contest their right to give the homily one usually notices that little or nothing has been done to recognize their gifts and their power to enlighten the congregation, and that the liturgy remains highly clerical.

It is for the mysteries and salvation of God proclaimed in the scriptures and effective in the life of the church that God is praised and thanked in sacrament, and it is in these mysteries that the community shares through its sacramental action. The one who proclaims the eucharistic prayer, or any other sacramental blessing, must be able to proclaim and interpret the scriptures for the community. To have a presider dispense the sacramental form, but take no part in the interpretation of the scriptures on which sacrament is based, is to pervert the liturgy and to destroy the unity between work and sacrament. A firm presidency, however, through which the interpretation of the word carries over into the proclamation of the blessing and the offer of the sacrament to the community, is quite compatible with a multiple exercise of charisms of proclamation and interpretation by other members of the community. Making room for this may disturb the neat ordering of epistle-response-gospel-homily-bidding prayers, but then the structure is a means to an end, not the end in itself. We are presently living in a period when the church has to explore all the different ways in which the members of a community can break the bread of God's word for one another, and then explore how these are to be integrated into liturgical celebration.

TRANSFORMING THE DAILY EXPERIENCE OF MINISTRY
Ministries do not flourish in liturgical celebration un-

179

less they flourish in the life of the community, or at least, once they begin to abound in liturgy, they provide a model for church life that must foster other services. It is up to liturgy as an act of God's people to integrate the mutual empowerment and service that goes on in a community of faith from day to day, and to express its sacramental meaning.

This point seems to be well illustrated by the nature of the deaconate. The service to the poor and to community administration that forms the role of the deacon in community life is given meaningful expression in the deacon's liturgical service at the altar. Bread for the community and bread for the Lord's supper come from the same earth and from the same hands, and must be ministered with the same care and love. The blessing that transforms the bread and wine into Christ's body and blood is an act of thanksgiving for the world's liberation through him and is done in the power of the same Spirit who gives birth to a communion in which all are members, one of another. This prayer, said by the presider in the name of the community, incorporates the deaconal service of the community, as represented in its ordained deacon. What needs to be brought out is that this service is indeed multiple and varied, and that it is not reducible to the activity or the gifts of the ordained deacon.

When, therefore, the issue of new liturgical ministries comes up, or in broader sense the relation of ministry to liturgy, one has to ask what are the new ways in which Christian people are empowering one another in the name of Christ on a day to day basis. It is these ways that are to be affirmed in the worship of God and that often will find a liturgical expression that is indicative of their meaning within Christ's mystery of salvation. This principle has to some extent been put into operation in the revision of the rites for the sick, for the catechumenate and adult ini-

180

tiation, and for marriage. Those who care for the bodily and mental needs of the sick, in the bonds of true personal relationships, are called upon to express the meaning of this service in the rites for the visitation of the sick, in the bringing to them of sacramental communion, and in the celebration of the sacrament of anointing. To some extent, this is an agenda that has been set rather than a common achievement in church life, but the way has been opened by the reforms, even if this is rather timidly done in the case of the sacrament of anointing itself, where it is still only the priest who is called upon to anoint and to lay on hands. Likewise, in the preparation of adults for baptism, the sponsors or the catechists have a specific liturgical ministry in the celebration of the rites, which expresses the nature of the bond between them and the candidates. The role of the witnesses in a blessing of a marriage by the church also clearly needs to be related to the part that they play in aiding the couple to come to a bonding in faith and to embark on a life of union together as woman and man. There are many social impediments to be overcome before this kind of agenda is put into practice, but at least the agenda is there.

Where an agenda is sadly lacking is in the case of the church's celebration of forgiveness and reconciliation, probably because we are still lacking a meaningful contemporary expression of where this sacrament has its place in the life of the faith community. The issue cannot be properly addressed if the ministry of sacramental reconciliation is reduced to the granting of absolution, and the need for the sacrament to the need to be absolved through the power of the keys. Such an expression of the sacrament's meaning ignores the full range of the exercise of the power of the keys, for one thing. This once meant the regulation of penance, with regard to its imposition, its inception, its moderation, and its termination. The penance was in-

tended to bring about that conversion of heart and
mores that would allow for full reconciliation with
God in the community of the church. The guidance of
spiritual persons and the support of all the people
were integral to the penitential process, and this was
affirmed and consolidated in a variety of liturgies.
The process of doing penance being less formal today, the guidance and support of fellow-believers is
being provided in many other ways. Ministries of forgiveness and reconciliation, in the opening up of con-
science, the healing of wounds and divisions, the
integration of the marginal into communal life, the
giving of spiritual direction, are numerous today
among the baptized, both men and women. What is
needed is a form of communal sacramental celebration in which the relation of these ministries to the
gift of God's reconciliation in Christ, through the
church and in the power of the Spirit, is recognized
and validated. The 1983 Synod of Bishops on Reconciliation took up the question, or at least some inter-
ventions were addressed to the point of the many
ministries involved, but it did not succeed in coming
to any fresh theological formulation, and still less to
any fresh forms of liturgical celebration. In the event,
the post-Synodal statement of Pope John Paul II broke
little new ground, and we may expect that the place
of penance in the life of the church will continue to
be agitated for some time. Certainly, it cannot be carried very far without closer enquiry into the ways in
which lay people have a part in the ministry of reconciliation and without arriving at some liturgical formulation that recognizes this.[4]

MUTUAL HOSPITALITY

A Christian community gathers together in a place of
worship. How they treat this place, how they relate to it,
how they see themselves reflected in it, how they look
out from it upon the world, none of this happens auto-
matically; it is effected by ministry within the body.

182

What is done in a place, makes the place. This is not to discount the contribution of art and architecture, nor to express indifference regarding the kind of place in which a worshiping community gathers. It is only to see them as subsidiary to action.

Some of the early places of Christian assembly have a note of domesticity which later edifices lack, but to which some communities now return. This is the case with the upper room, the catacombs, or the house at Dura Europos, as it is with the mud or brick churches of lowly hamlets where basic Christian communities gather in the intimacy of their poverty as well as of their hope. The domesticity comes in part from the place's extreme simplicity, but it is further suggested by the kind of action which it is likely to house. The services of mutual hospitality which belong in such a place are these: to wash one another's feet, to comfort the ill and the afflicted, to be open-armed to the stranger, to share the common food and drink of the Body and the Blood in the forms of bread and wine.

Some of the services rendered in the type of gathering envisaged here are those expected of the acolyte, the usher, the ministers of communion, or other hospitalers. The service they are asked to show to others in the community is of the essence of Christian gathering. Something more is asked of them, however, and that is the grace to dispose the place and use the things of ritual in such a way as to "let things speak." This is of the beauty of liturgy.

The things put to use in Christian worship are very simple: bread, wine, a table, oil, water, a clean vessel, a burning candle. We tend not to *hear* them, nor to *see* them, clouding their appearance and their voice with words such as Body, Blood, real presence, sacrifice, etc. True though these dogmatic formulas are, there is a way of using them which conceals reality. We cannot truly seize what it is to receive the Body and the Blood of the

Lord, or to be forgiven in God's mercy, or to be assisted in illness, unless we see the things first for what they are, rather than for what dogma says of them. It is when they are perceived for what they are in themselves that they take us outside of the place in which we gather and put us in tune with the universe as macrocosm and as microcosm. Paradoxically, a place of gathering where there is reverence for bread and wine, oil and water, and a readiness to listen to them speak, is a central point radiating holiness to the entire cosmos.

Christian people minister to one another in liturgy in such a way as to express Christ's coming among them in the simplicity and the power of fragile but eloquent things like carafes of wine, wheaten cakes, freshly drawn water, or the oil that flows into the beard and on to the limbs. Naturally, care about such things and the life that goes with them belongs in daily life, but the care is expressed in worship in a prayer of faith. Through such care, humanity learns to live in new ways on the earth and under the skies, doing so with the example before its eyes of Jesus washing the feet of his disciples, breaking bread for the crowds, pouring wine for a young married couple, and laying gentle hands on the paralytic and the epileptic.

CONCLUSION
The services that Christians render to one another in the word, in mutual hospitality, and in other forms of empowerment are given multiple expression in the liturgy and give rise to a variety of specific liturgical ministries. Many of these ministries can be rendered by one and all, and simply need care and supervision to be done well. Reading is a common skill today. Giving communion to one another, or carrying home the Lord's Body to family members or friends, is not to be done disrespectfully, but it is surely a character-istic of any Christian that she or he can approach and handle the Body of Christ. Being an usher or looking

after the collection are not unusual services, requireing unusual gifts, although they demand politeness, gentleness, and honesty. By and large, there seems little reason to make such services stand out as extraordinary or needful of special qualities and appointment.

Other ministries require special skills and training. Music direction, the spiritual guidance of others, teaching, prayer in public, prophecy, involve the careful and well-prepared use of special gifts and skills. In regard to such, there is room for a discernment and for the kind of recognition suggested in the preceding chapter. It is to this aspect of ministry that our attention is drawn by Paul VI in the reforms that he enacted to meet the Council's desire for a full, active, and varied participation of the faithful in the liturgy, so that as a holy and elect people they might minister to the world in Christ's name, in the power of the Spirit, for the eternal glory of the Father.

NOTES

1. See Eduard Cothenet, "La Première Epitre de Pierre," *Le Ministère et les Ministères selon le Nouveau Testament*, 138-151.

2. Canon 230, par. 3.

3. For a discussion of the issue, cf. the following works: *Preaching and the Non-Ordained. An Interdisciplinary Study*, edited by Nadine Foley (Liturgical Press, Collegeville 1983); J. Frank Henderson, "The Minister of Liturgical Preaching," *Worship* 56 (1982) 214–230; William Skudlarek, "Lay Preaching and the Liturgy," *Worship* 58 (1984) 500–506.

4. Some helpful orientations may be found in Robert J. Hater, "Sin and Reconciliation: Changing Attitudes in the Catholic Church," *Worship* 59 (1985) 18–31. For an analysis of John Paul's post-Synodal exhortation in relation to the Synod's discussions, cf. James Dallen, "Reconciliatio et Paenitentia: The Postsynodal Apostolic Exhortation," *Worship* 59 (1985) 98–116.

Conclusion

In changing the discipline concerning minor orders, and providing for a formal recognition of some lay ministries in the church, Paul VI showed the church's desire to follow up on the steps taken at the Second Vatican Council. By linking this recognition with the given canonical rulings, these provisions imposed restrictions on lay ministry even while recognizing its legitimacy. The nature, scope, and source of this ministry are too narrowly defined in the provisions made. The facts of lay ministry go far beyond what was accounted for in *Ministeria quaedam*, and history and current practice both indicate that further developments are desirable and possible. The way has been opened, the work of the Spirit will continue.

In this study, I have sought throughout to relate the question of ministry to community renewal, rather than to any abstract notion of church. I have also shown, in the light of history, practice, and theological reflection, that what is at stake is not simply the addition or emergence of a few new ministries, nor simply an increase in the number of involved laity. Church ministry is taking an entirely new shape before our eyes, one that configures much more accurately the symbol of the eschatological people, called in the Spirit, proclaimed in the New Testament as God's new creation in his Son, Jesus Christ, our Lord and the world's Redeemer.

Bibliography

SOURCES: ANCIENT AND MEDIEVAL

Constitutions of the Holy Apostles, translated and edited with notes by J. Donaldson, *The Ante-Nicene Fathers*, vol. 7. Charles Scribner's Sons, New York 1925.

Didascalia Apostolorum, the Syriac version translated and accompanied by the Verona Latin fragments, with an introduction and notes by R.H. Connolly. Clarendon Press, Oxford 1929.

Eusebius' Ecclesiastical History, translated from the original with an introduction by C.F. Cruse. Baker Book House, Grand Rapids, Michigan 1977.

Liber Sacramentorum Romanae Aeclesiae Ordinis Anni Circuli (Sacramentarium Gelasium), ed. L. C. Mohlberg. Herder, Rome 1960.

Missale Francorum, ed. L.C. Mohlberg. Herder, Rome 1957.

Les Ordines Romani du Haut Moyen Age, ed. M. Andrieu. Spicilegium Sacrum Lovaniense, Louvain 1931-1956, 4 vols.

Le Pontifical Romano-Germanique du Dixième Siècle, vol. 1, ed. C. Vogel and R. Elze. Biblioteca Apostolica Vaticana, Vatican City 1963.

Les Statuta Ecclesiae Antiqua, ed. Ch. Munier. Presse Universitaire de France, Paris 1960.

The Testament of the Lord, ed. J. Cooper and A.J. MacLean. T. & T. Clark, Edinburgh 1902.

La Tradition Apostolique de Saint Hippolyte, essai de reconstitution par Dom Bernard Botte. Aschendorf, Münster 1963.

187

The Treatise on the Apostolic Tradition of St. Hippolytus of Rome, edited by Gregory Dix, reissued with corrections, preface, and bibliography by Henry Chadwick. SPCK, London 1968.

SOURCES: CONTEMPORARY MAGISTERIUM
Assemblée Plénière de l'Episcopat Français. *Tous Responsables dans l'Eglise?* Le Centurion, Paris 1973.

Association of Member Episcopal Conferences in East Africa (AMECEA). "Building Christian Community." *African Ecclesiastical Review* 18 (1976) 249-258.

Bishops' Committee on the Liturgy. *Study Text 1: Holy Communion. Commentary on the Instruction Immensae Caritatis*. United States Catholic Conference, Washington, D.C. 1973.

————. *Study Text 3: Ministries in the Church. Commentary on the Apostolic Letters of Pope Paul VI Ministeria Quaedam and Ad Pascendum.* United States Catholic Conference; Washington, D.C. 1974.

Commission Episcopale Française de la Liturgie. "Note de la Commission." *Documentation Catholique* 67 (1970) 311-317.

Conférence Episcopale Allemande. "Communiqué du rapporteur de la Conférence: Les Prédicateurs Laics." *Documentation Catholique* 70 (1973) 108i.

————. "La Participation des Laics à la Prédication en Allemagne Fédérale." *Documentation Catholique* 71 (1974) 645-646.

————. "Le Prêtre, le Diacre et le Laic dans la Pastorale." *Documentation Catholique* 74 (1977) 517-522.

Conferenza Episcopale Italiana. "Evangelizzazione e Sacramenti: Documento Pastorale dei Vescovi Italiana." *Il Regno: Documentazione* 18 (1973) 396-405.

————. "I Ministeri nella Chiesa: Documento Pastorale." *Notiziario CEI* 8 (1973) 157-168.

Conselho Permanente da CNBB. "Comunidades Ecclesiais de Base," *Comunicado Mensal: Conferencia Nalcional dos Bispos de Brasil.* Novembre de 1982, no. 362, 1180–1195.

General Secretariate for the Synod of Bishops. "The Laity's Vocation and Mission," *Origins* 14 (1985) 624–634.

John Paul II. "Address to the Synod Secretariate," *Origins* 14 (1984) 148f.

―――. "The Laity's Call to Serve," *Origins* 14 (1984) 255f.

Paul VI. *On Evangelization in the Modern World*. United States Catholic Conference, Washington, D.C. 1976.

The Rites of the Catholic Church as Revised by Decree of the Second Vatican Council and Published by Authority of Pope Paul VI, English translation prepared by the International Commission on English in the Liturgy. Pueblo Publishing Co., New York 1976.

Sacred Congregation for the Discipline of the Sacraments. *Instruction Fidei Custos on Extraordinary Ministers of Eucharistic Communion*, private circulation. A French translation is given in *Documentation Catholique* 67 (1970) 310-316.

―――. "Instruction Empowering Lay Persons to Preside at Marriage in Brazil." *Doctrine and Life* 25 (1975) 670-672.

Third General Conference of Latin American Bishops. *Evangelization at Present and in the Future of Latin America: Conclusions*. National Conference of Catholic Bishops, Washington, D.C. 1979.

"U.S. Bishops Pastoral Letter on Hispanic Ministry," *Origins* 13 (1984) 529-541.

Vatican Council II: the Conciliar and Post-Conciliar Documents, ed. A. Flannery. Costello Publishing Co., Northport, New York 1977.

LITERATURE
Augé, M. "El Sacramento del Orden segun los Concilios Espanoles de los Siglos IV-VII." *Claretianum* 5 (1965) 71-93.

"Asian Colloquium on Ministries: Conclusion." *Origins* 8 (1978) 129-143.

Basic Christian Communities in the Church. *Pro Mundi Vita* 62 (1976).

Béraudy, R. "Les Ministères Institués dans 'Ministeria Quaedam' et 'Ad Pascendum.'" *La Maison-Dieu* 115 (1973) 86-96.

Bissonette, T. "Comunidades Eclesiales de Base: Some Con-

189

temporary Attempts to Build Ecclesial Koinonia." *The Jurist* 36 (1976) 24-58.

Bittlinger, A. *Gifts and Ministries.* W.B. Eerdmans Publishing Co., Grand Rapids 1973.

Blessings and Consecrations. A Book of Occasional Services. United Methodist Church Supplemental Worship Resources 14 (Abingdon Press, Nashville 1984).

Botte, B. "Confessor." *Archivium Latinitatis Medii Aevi* 16 (1941) 137-154.

———. "L'Ordination du Lecteur dans le Pontifical Romain." *Questions Liturgiques et Paroissiales* 24 (1939) 36-37.

———. "Le Problème des Ordres Mineurs." *Questions Liturgiques et Paroissiales* 46 (1965) 26-31.

———. "Le Rituel d'Ordination des Statuta Ecclesiae Antiqua." *Recherches de Théologie Ancienne et Médiévale* 11 (1939) 223-241.

———. "Le Traité des Charismes dans les 'Constitutions Apostoliques.'" *Studia Patristica* XII (1975) 83-86,

Braga, C. "Ministeria Quaedam." *Ephemerides Liturgicae* 87 (1973) 191-214.

"Brasilia: Relatorio sobre os Ministérios Litúrgicos Exercidos por Leigos." *Notitiae* 11 (1975) 263-268.

Bussini, F. "Les Eglises et leurs Ministères." *La Maison-Dieu* 115 (1973) 107-132.

Cé, M. "Ministeri Istituiti e Ministeri Straordinari." *Il Regno: Documentazione* 21 (1976) 266-271.

Charisms in the Church, ed. C. Floristan and C. Duquoc, *Concilium* 109. Seabury Press, New York 1978.

Coffey, R. and R. Varro. *Eglise Signe de Salut au Milieu des Hommes: Eglise-Sacrement,* Rapports présentés à l'Assemblée Plénière de l'Episcopat Français, Lourdes 1971. Le Centurion, Paris 1972.

"Commentarium de Nova Disciplina et de Ritibus circa Ministeria." *Notitiae* 9 (1973) 18-33.

Conférences Saint-Serge. *L'Assemblée Liturgique et les Différents*

190

Rôles dans l'Assemblée. XXIIIe Semaine d'Etudes Liturgiques, 1976. Ed. Liturgiche, Rome 1977. (English trans., *Roles in the Liturgical Assembly.* Pueblo Publishing Co., New York 1981.)

Congar, Y. *Jalons Pour Une Théologie du Laicat.* Ed. du Cerf, Paris 1953 (English trans., *Lay People in the Church.* The Newman Press, Westminster, Md., revised edition 1967.)

————. *Ministères et Communion Ecclésiale.* Ed. du Cerf, Paris 1971.

————. "My Path-findings in the Theology of Laity and Ministries." *The Jurist* 32 (1972) 169-188.

Coppenrath, J. "Les Ordres Inférieurs: Degrés de Sacerdoce ou Etapes vers le Prêtrise?" *Nouvelle Revue Théologique* 81 (1959) 489-501.

Coriden, J. "Laying the Groundwork for Further Ministries." *Origins* 4 (1974) 401-410.

————. "Ministries for the Future." *Studia Canonica* 8 (1974) 255-275.

Croce, W. "Die niederen Weihe und ihre hierarchische Wertung." *Zeitschrift für katholische Theologie* 70 (1948) 257-314.

Cummins, J. "Report at Congress of Presidents and Secretaries of National Liturgical Commissions, October 23–28, 1984," *Origins* 14 (1984) 400–405.

Davies, J.G. "Deacons, Deaconesses and Minor Orders in the Patristic Period." *Journal of Ecclesiastical History* 14 (1963) 1-15.

Dictionnaire d'Archéologie Chrétienne et de Liturgie, articles "Acolyte," "Exorciste," "Fossoyers," "Lecteur," "Portier," "Psalmiste."

Didier, R. "Le Ministre Extraordinaire de la Distribution de la Communion. Note Historique et Théologique." *La Maison-Dieu* 103 (1970) 73-85.

Discernment of the Spirit and of Spirits, ed. C. Floristan and C. Duquoc, *Concilium* 119. Seabury Press, New York 1979.

Dussel, E. "The Differentiation of Charisms." In *Charisms in the Church*, ed. C. Floristan and C. Duquoc, *Concilium* 109. Seabury Press, New York 1977.

Faivre, A. *Naissance d'une Hiérarchie: Les Premières Etapes du Cursus Clérical*. Ed. Beauchesne, Paris 1977.

Fedwick, P.J. *The Church and the Charisma of Leadership in Basil of Caesarea*. Pontifical Institute of Medieval Studies, Toronto 1979.

Fischer, B. "Der Niedere Klerus bei Gregor der Grosse." *Zeitschrift für katholische Theologie* 62 (1938) 37-75.

————. "Esquisse Historique sur les Ordres Mineurs." *La Maison-Dieu* 61 (1961) 5-29.

Foley, N. (ed.). *Preaching and the Non-Ordained. An Interdisciplinary Study* (Liturgical Press, Collegeville 1983).

Galilea, S. "Liberation as an Encounter with Politics and Contemplation." In *The Mystical and Political Dimension of the Christian Faith*, ed. C. Geffré and G. Gutierrez, *Concilium* 96, 19-33. Herder & Herder, New York 1974.

Gaspar, M. *What is the Mindanao-Sulu Pastoral Conference?* No date or place.

Goldie, R. "Lay, Laity, Laicity: A Bibliographical Survey of Three Decades," *The Laity Today: Bulletin of the Pontifical Council of the Laity* 26 (1979) 107-143.

Gryson, R. *The Ministry of Women in the Early Church*. Liturgical Press, Collegeville 1976.

Guimarâes, A.R. "Comunidades de Base—Busca de Equilibrio entre Ministérios e Comunidade Cristâ." *Revista Eclesiástica Brasileria* 38 (1978) 80-102.

Hasenhuttl, G. *Charisma Ordnungsprinzip der Kirche*. Herder, Freiburg 1969.

Hastings, A. *Church and Ministry*. Gaba Publication, Kampala 1972.

Hemrick, Eugene, "Report on Church Personnel: Developments in Ministry," *Origins* 13 (1984) 561-566.

Henderson, F. *Ministries of the Laity*. Canadian Conference of Catholic Bishops, Ottawa 1978.

Henderson, J. F. "The Ministry of Liturgical Preaching," *Worship* 56 (1982) 214-230.

Hoornaert, E. "Comunidades de Base—Dez Anos de Experiência." *Revista Eclesiástica Brasileira* 38 (1978) 474-502.

Hovda, R. *There are Different Ministries*. Liturgical Conference, Washington D.C. 1975.

Huels, J. M. "Female Altar Servers: The Legal Issue," *Worship* 57 (1983) 513–525. *Occasional Services*, prepared by the Churches participating in the Inter-Lutheran Commission on Worship (Augsburg Press, Minneapolis 1982).

"Immensae Caritatis—Commentarium." *Notitiae* 9 (1973) 168-173.

Kavanagh, A. *The Shape of Baptism: The Rite of Christian Initiation*. Pueblo Publishing Co., New York 1978.

Keller, M. "Theologie des Laientums." In J. Feiner and M. Löhrer, *Mysterium Salutis* 4/2, 393-421. Benziger Verlag, Einsiedeln 1973.

Kilmartin, E. "A Modern Approach to the Word of God and Sacraments of Christ: Perspectives and Principles." In *The Sacraments: God's Mercy Actualized*, ed. F. Eigo, 59-109. Villanova University Press, Villanova 1979.

"La Question des Ministères en Afrique: Dossier." *Spiritus* 18 (1977) 339-364.

Lavardière, L. "Evolution et Révolution Pastorales en Afrique Centrale." *Revue du Clergé Africain* 27 (1972) 177-200.

Le Ministère et les Ministères selon le Nouveau Testament: Dossier Exégétique et Réflexion Théologique, ed. J. Delorme. Ed. du Seuil, Paris, 1974.

Lécuyer, J. "Les Ordres Mineurs en Question." *La Maison-Dieu* 102 (1970) 97-107.

Legrand, H.-M. "The Presidency of the Eucharist According to the Ancient Tradition." *Worship* 53 (1979) 413-438.

———. "Ministries: Main Lines of Research in Catholic Theology." *Pro Mundi Vita* 50 (1974) 7-16.

Lemaire, A. "Ministères et Eucharistie aux Origines de l'Eglise." *Spiritus* 18 (1977) 386-398.

———. "The Ministries in the New Testament: Recent Research." *Biblical Theology Bulletin* 3 (1973) 133-166.

Lobinger, F. *How Much Can Lay People Do?* Lumko Institute, Lady Frere, South Africa 1973.

Ministries in the Church in India, ed. D.S. Amalorpavadass. Research Seminar and Pastoral Consultation, C.B.C.I. Centre, New Delhi, 1976.

Moingt, J. "Services et Lieux d'Eglise." *Etudes* 350 (1979/1) 835-850; 351 (1979/2) 103-120, 363-394.

Montcheuil, Y. de. *Aspects of the Church*, trans. A. Lamothe. Fides, Chicago 1955.

New Forms of Ministries in Christian Communities. Pro Mundi Vita 50 (1974).

Nikolasch, F. "Die Neuordnung der Kirchlichen Dienste." *Liturgische Jahrbuch* 22 (1972) 169-182.

Notebaart, J. "Start-Off Rites for Religious Ed: Liturgies to Recognize Catechists." *Liturgy* 24/5 (1979) 13-14.

O'Meara, T. *Theology of Ministry* (Paulist Press, New York 1983).

Parrett, J.-K. "The Laying-On of Hands in the New Testament." *Expository Times* 80 (1969) 210-214.

Potterie, I. de la. "L'Origine et le Sens Primitif du mot 'Laic.'" *Nouvelle Revue Théologique* 80 (1958) 840-853.

Rahner, K. "Note on the Lay Apostolate." In *Theological Investigations* 2, 319-352. Helicon Press, Baltimore 1963.

Ranasinghe, L. "Rethinking Ministries: at the Service of Uva Province." In *Beyond Rite to Reality*, 85-96. Sevaka Sevana Publications 2, Columbo, Sri Lanka 1976.

Reynolds, R. *The Ordinals of Christ from their Origins to the Twelfth Century*. Walter de Gruyter, Berlin-New York 1978.

Ruspi, W. "I Ministeri Istituiti nella Interpretazione di alcune Chiese Locali." *Revista Liturgica* 63 (1976) 629-640.

Skudlarek, W. "Lay Preaching and the Liturgy," *Worship* 58 (1984) 500-506.

Sottocornola, F. "Significato e Funzione dei Ministeri Laici Nell'Assemblea Liturgica." *Rivista Liturgica* 63 (1976) 641-651.

Snuders, A. "Acolytus cum Ordinatur: Eine Historische Studie." *Sacris Erudiri* 9 (1957) 163-198.

Sobrino, J. "Following Jesus as Discernment." In *Discernment of the Spirit and of Spirits*, ed. C. Floristan and C. Duquoc, *Concilium* 119, 14-24. Seabury Press, New York 1979.

Socha, H. "Die 'Dienstämter' des Lektors und Akolythen." *Münchener Theologische Zeitschrift* 25 (1974) 138-151.

The Churches of Africa: Future Prospects, ed. C. Geffré and B. Luneau, *Concilium* 106. Seabury Press, New York 1977.

The Parish in Community and Ministry, edited and introduced by Evelyn Eaton Whitehead. Paulist Press, New York 1978.

Touchstones for Liturgical Ministries, ed. V. Sloyan. Liturgical Conference, Washington, D.C. 1978.

Urdeix, J. "Presente y Futuro del Lector y del Acólito," *Phase* 15 (1975) 435-452.

Vanhoye, A. "Sacerdoce Commun et Sacerdoce Ministèriel: Distinction et Rapports." *Nouvelle Revue Théologique* 97 (1975) 193-207.

Van Beneden, P. *Aux Origines d'une Terminologie Sacramentelle: Ordo, Ordinare, Ordinatio dans la Littérature Chrétienne avant 313.* Spicilegium Sacrum Lovaniense, Louvain 1974.

Vancelles, L. de. "L'Avenir des Communautés et des Ministères dans le Catholicisme Français," *Etudes* 340 (1974/1) 109-121.

Vinel, A. "L'Instruction Immensae Caritatis," *La Maison-Dieu* 114 (1973) 110-113.

Zevini, G. "The Christian Initiation of Adults into the Neo-Catechumenal Community." In *Structures of Initiation in Crisis*, ed. L. Maldonado and D. Power, *Concilium* 122, 65-74. Seabury Press, New York 1979.

Index

202